TWELVE DAYS IN THE OZARKS

A Personal Diary

Robert Leon Kennedy

Wilmar House Publishing
P. O. Box 1714
Branson, Mo. 65616

Copyright © 1990 Robert Leon Kennedy
Second Printing

A special thanks to:

Rex A. Bohm, State of Missouri Department of Natural Resources,
Taneyhills Library and staff,
The School of the Ozarks Library and staff,
Branson/Lakes Area Chamber of Commerce,
Missouri Department of Conservation,
U.S. Army Corps of Engineers,
Ms. Bonnie Thompson, cover design
Ms. Wendy Mohling, page design and typesetting.

Day One
November 11

Morning Communion

Communion:
1. A Sharing; possesion is common.
2. A communing; sharing of one's thoughts and emotions.
3. An intimate spiritual relationship.
4. A sharing in, or celebration of the eucharist. [1]

The sound of the wall heater kicking on rouses me from a comfortable sleep. Slowly opening my eyes, I see the room aglow in early morning sunlight.

Morning is a lazy time for me since my body is more nocturnal by nature. I can spend whole mornings letting consciousness re-enter this mind that has been dominated by dreams and the unseen workings of the subconscious.

In the early morning coolness, amphibians lie motionless on rocks, waiting for the sun's warming rays to revive their bodies' life forces. I lie motionless underneath my warm patchwork quilts; half asleep, half awake, waiting.

This is the perfect place to be on a Saturday morning in November. November 11th to be exact; Veterans' Day. No place in particular to go, and nothing of importance to do.

I roll over and look at the clock which reads 7:34 a.m. Maybe a little more sleep would be in order.

This thought quickly vanishes as the sound of geese reaches my ears. Not the distant honking of migrating flocks passing high overhead on their annual pilgrimage to the warmer lands to the south, but very loud, boisterous calls from just outside. This is my wake-up call.

Slowly getting out of my warm bed, I straighten the bed clothes as I go. This is an old military habit that hasn't

---

[1]. Webster's New World Dictionary of the American Language.

been abandoned even after all these years of being a civilian again. It's a good habit. I find it easier to face a new day already having finished a bit of work before my feet are solidly on the floor. It also discourages me from going back to bed, since I would have to mess up the neat bed covers to do so.

I stumble to the kitchen and put on a pot of coffee. A quick shower washes the sleep from my eyes. After drying off, I run a comb through my hair and brush my teeth, heading back to the kitchen to check on the coffee.

Indoor plumbing. It, along with electricity, gas furnaces, and the other conveniences of modern life are taken for granted. This morning I didn't have to open the flue on the old, black cast iron wood stove. There was no fumbling with the iron poker in an attempt to stir the coals in the bottom of the stove back to life, rekindling a smoky fire. There was no water carried in a bucket from the spring at the bottom of the hill. No cold chamber pot, or sabbatical to the wooden privy behind the house. No coffee boiled over the smoky stove in a bulky kettle.

Yes, for many, including myself, things have changed drastically in the last 50 or so years. But even so, this is still "the hills," "the woods," "the sticks," or any of a dozen other colloquialisms. To me, it's just home. This is the Ozark Mountains.

The coffee is ready. The smell is as stimulating to my nose as the first taste of the steaming cup is to my tongue. The aroma fills the room as I fill a stone mug with the black liquid.

Ah! Good morning! My day is never properly started until that first cup of stimulant. My obvious addiction to coffee is not purely physical, for I'm sure there are deep psychological foundations as well.

Coffee, in my developing years, was the social drink of our family. Often the enticing smell of freshly brewed coffee filled our home. Every weekday afternoon at 4:30, my dad would come home from the daily stress and physical abuse that comes from long hours of standing on concrete, doing methodical, redundant motions on the assembly line. The coffee was symbolic of a return to real life.

Even now I can't go home for a visit without the "Mr. Coffee" being pressed into service almost immediately upon my arrival.

With the caffeine quickly entering my system, I am ready for the day. So I slip into a pair of jeans, a T-shirt, and my trusty, well worn tennis shoes.

Opening the curtains, I look out into the morning. There's a heavy frost on the ground; the first hard frost of the season. This is really pretty late for it, but the jet stream that's been holding the colder weather to the north has finally slipped southward, bringing more normal temperatures with it. Trees that are often bare by this time are still going through the annual color change that the Ozarks is so famous for.

There was a lot of rain in October that kept things unseasonably green, and when nature's clock finally signaled the deciduous trees to slow down their sap flow, the leaves began turning incredible colors, the prettiest I've seen in years.

This color, much of which is always there, but hidden by the green chlorophyll, is the great finale of summer. I wonder how many times this color change has taken place in the forests? How many eyes have witnessed it, the great unveiling?

Slipping on a flannel shirt and a down-filled vest, snapping it up tight, I refill my mug with hot coffee, open the door and step out.

The 26 degree air welcomes me abruptly. My skin reacts to the sharp slap of cold, and I take a quick deep breath.

I am awake!

The frost covers the grass below the balcony, and glistens as the early morning sun reflects off it. The railing of the balcony is also coated in the icy crystals and I feel a chill as I brush my hand over it.

I walk along the balcony to where it looks out over North Beach Park , and beyond it to Lake Taneycomo. My nostrils are still reacting to the sensation of very cold air passing through them.

An early morning mist lies motionless above the lake, making it almost invisible.

A few feet below me, moving about in the glistening grass, is the flock of wild Canadian geese that announced its arrival earlier, and that has kept up the honking since. They seem to be everywhere.

I try to count them, but they are constantly moving, so it takes me three times to get an estimate of 70. These wild birds are beautiful, even though wild is not totally accurate. They've taken up permanent residence on this lake, like many other waterfowl, and have grown somewhat accustomed to people, eagerly accepting handouts of bread, popcorn, and cheese puffs. Sometimes they seem to be more like pets.

The local residents along Lake Taneycomo are very protective of these geese. This was greatly emphasized by the amount of public outcry at an announcement by the Missouri Department of Conservation that open goose hunting would be allowed on the lake.

Nature has a very precise way of doing business. It has established a balance in its ecosystems; prey and predator, plant and animal. When this balance is altered by some happening, all parts of the system are altered accordingly, until there is a balance again. Each alteration is for the good of the species and the ecosystem, not the individual. And this is good for all of nature.

But man has a preoccupation with morality, and too often lacks a real understanding about that morality, so he is totally lost when it comes to dealing with an amoral system, as is nature. In this regard, man seems to be a counter-productive mutation in the evolutionary chain. I'm often as guilty as anyone.

In an uncontrolled environment, if these geese overpopulate, so will their predators. We control their predators, of which we are one. Also, if they overpopulate, the food supplies decrease, and they starve. I stand on the balcony and throw them day old bread.

These beautiful creatures give me such pleasure. Majestic beggars; sacred cows. They are totally unaware of the furor that their presence has created, and contentedly eat their breakfast of bread and frost covered grass. The legal battle wages on.

I watch them eat for a while and then look back to the serenity of the mist enshrouded lake. Lake Taneycomo, such an exotic sounding name. When I first heard it, I was sure that it was of Indian origin. It was a bit disappointing when I discovered it was only an acronym for *Taney County, Missouri*; Taneycomo.

Taney County got its name from Roger Brooke Taney who was the attorney general under President Andrew Jackson (1829-1837). At first it covered an extremely large area, but eventually was divided into many counties and this one kept the original name.

This lake was formed by the construction of Powersite Dam, at Ozark Beach, in 1913. It lies about 15 miles east of here, and was the first dam built on the White River.

The dam changed this primitive, backwoods area into one of increased social and economic development by bringing electricity into the White River region.

This lake, for many years, was a popular spot for camping, boating, and water recreation, as well as for fishing.

Powersite Dam was built, in part, to help with flood control on the river, but even after it was built, the area still had flood problems. The Federal Flood Control Act of 1938 was designed to eliminate such a danger. However, the project was delayed due to a lack of funds during World War II and the Korean War. The last two major floods occurred here in 1943 and 1945.

Table Rock Dam project was finally initiated in the early 1950's about eight miles west of Branson and went on line in 1959.

The new dam, much larger than Powersite, is made up of over a million and a quarter cubic yards of concrete. It is 6,423 feet long, and at full capacity can process six million gallons of water per minute. Behind the dam formed Table Rock Lake, whose 43,100 acres greatly dwarf Lake Taneycomo.

The water that is released from the bottom of Table Rock into Taneycomo lowered the temperature of Taneycomo. This greatly curtailed swimming and skiing on this lake, but it also inadvertently created a perfect environment for trout, *salmonidae.*

Taking advantage of this, a trout hatchery was built at the base of Table Rock Dam. Its main purpose is to raise the fingerling rainbow and brown trout that are used to restock Taneycomo and surrounding spring-fed streams. The hatchery releases approximately 40,000 six-inch trout into the cold lake waters every month.

Some of these small trout fall victim to the predations of other fish or birds or turtles. However, many survive, growing quickly on the supply of insects and crustaceans, eventually to become a meal for a hungry eagle or fisherman.

The early morning calm frames the sound of a small boat chugging along the lake. In the rear of the boat, with one hand on the motor's guide arm, while steering his craft upstream, rides a lone fisherman who is either returning from a pre-dawn excursion or is moving to another fishing spot somewhere beyond the city campgrounds.

Fishermen are a breed of people unto themselves. They seem totally unaffected by the cold or wet or wind. Often they can be seen riding up and down the lake, or placidly sitting on the bank in a portable aluminum lawn chair, in the dead of winter. With the temperature well below freezing, and the wind chill dangerously low, their gloved hands are wrapped around the rod handle, waiting for a telegraphic signal of success. They seem undaunted by the cold, or the coating of ice that has formed on the line, and has all but frozen the eyelets of the rod solid and inoperable. Such steadfast determination.

Here on my scenic view I too am communing with the same nature that the fisherman is, sharing his noble cause. But here, only a few feet from warmth, and a still half full pot of coffee, I lack some of his zeal and commitment.

The quiet beauty of the lake returns, as the last chugs from the motor fades away. Looking out on this enchanting scene, I wonder how many similar mornings have come and gone through time, and how many other eyes have witnessed such beauty.

I've read several books about this Ozarks Region and the myriad of happenings that have occurred here. This place is vastly rich with history, and I feel a bit sad when I think about the millions of people that pass through here annually on vacation, and even those who live here permanently, who never really get to know the Ozarks.

These hills have a strong hold on me, and I feel so honored to live here.

Along this White River Basin lived herds of buffalo, white deer, called Wapiti by the Indians, and even the mastadon. Also, raccoon, beaver, armadillo, musk ox, tapir, fish, wild turkey, numerous waterfowl, peccarie, squirrel, rabbit, and shellfish, among others. Along with an overabundance of flora, this area has proven to be a rich hunting ground for man, as well as the dire wolf, bear, mountain lion, and, at one time, even crocodilian.

The White River Valley is loaded with archeological sites filled with evidence to support this. Man has lived in this area for at least 14,000 years. From the paleo-Indian period up to the present, the Ozarks has been a good host to man.

Finding an arrowhead or a spear point might be a sign

that you've come upon a spot where a group of pre-historic Indians killed a giant mastadon, or buffalo, or wapiti. Or it might be the site of a battle between two warring tribes. The stone holds its secrets well.

Of all the Indian groups that have lived in or traveled through this land the Osage tribe is the most interesting to me.

The super race, the perfect race, and racial superiority has been a common ideology shared by many people in many times. The concept brings thoughts of the Spartans, or the ancient Greeks, or the Romans, or even Adolf Hitler and his plans for the master race; his belief in breeding a superior people. There are many accounts of such designed societies.

However, I was quite surprised when reading of how the Osage practiced this same ideology. The Osage were regarded as almost giants, since they averaged over six feet in height. To them this height was a sign of social prominence and strength. They were a very proud people, feeling superior to all others, white or Indian, and fought both with fervor, boasting of more enemies than any other tribe.

The practice of selective breeding was a part of the tribal plan for their superior race, to insure tall, fierce, physically beautiful people.

Only the bravest warriors were allowed to sire young. Should a young man fail to show courage in his first campaign, he was denegrated to the position of squaw man, wearing a squaw's clothing, and not allowed to marry for fear that his cowardice would be passed to his offspring.*

When a "not-so-tall" brave came looking for a bride, maidens were hidden away by their mothers, who would allow only the tallest men to become their sons-in-law.

Should an acceptable brave claim a maiden, he also laid claim to all her sisters, and from them would come many generations with the favorable traits.

---

* Some historians state that these MI-XU-GA were not being punished for cowardice, but were highly respected, having chosen their transvestite lifestyle after having a powerful vision or dream. They were thought to have the gift of prophecy.

Inbreeding was avoided by prohibiting any man from marrying within his clan. Also, the use of alcohol was prohibited by the elders who often met in the Lodge of Mystery to plan and evaluate the progress of their master race. They concluded that harsh drink caused insanity and would destroy their plan.

The Osage lived along the Ni-U-Skah, or White River, for many generations. They finally relinquished their jealous hold on this land when they signed the Treaty of 1808. But since they didn't understand the concept of owning land, they thought little of the treaty, and raided the whites and other Indian tribes that were moving into the area.

Their final raid came in 1823 when Mad Buffalo led a murderous assault on a camp of American and French men. The Osage warriors were eventually captured, and their leader, Mad Buffalo, along with one other, was put to death. The rest were pardoned and sent back west. Thus ended the reign of the Osage on the White River Valley, and ended the belief of a master race in the Ozarks; at least for a while.

Looking down at the park and the area around it, I can see that this would have been a good location for a village. The park runs parallel to the lake, ending abruptly at a cove on the north. This cove meets the lake at the point where Roark Creek emptied into the White River. Indian camps were often built near this type of setting. I close my eyes and imagine:

I can see several bow shelters covered with skins. These structures are made with long poles, sharpened on each end and both stuck into the ground, forming an arch. Three or four poles are used to frame these circular shelters. The poles are tied together at the intersecting point and hides are stretched over them.

A hazy smoke hangs over the village in the cool morning air. Indian children play a running game. Two squaws are cooking something over an open fire. A dog is lying nearby, intently gnawing at a remnant of a recent kill. Another dog tries to steal the prize, but the first dog successfully fends it off. There are about ten huts in the central part of the camp, with a larger one, the chief's hut, overlooking the others from a small hill. **

Off from the village is a larger, more elongated dwelling. It is the Lodge of Mystery, used for special ceremonies and meetings by the council.

The White River below the village meanders along the valley, past the high bluffs on the east, roaring over the shallows and gravel bars, and then widening into deep, quiet pools, until it reaches the next shallows.

A water snake works its way along the bank searching for an early morning meal of frog or fish that might be hiding among the exposed roots that are growing along the bank.

A swarm of mosquitoes swirl in a large column a few feet above the water at a point where warm sunlight breaks through the trees up on the cliffs above the river, and streams down to the water below.

There is a splash in the shadows along the far bank as a fish breaks the water's surface while chasing a meal.

In the distance a lone brave slowly, methodically paddles his canoe into the distance. He might be going on a hunt or checking on fish traps made out of tree limbs and placed along in the shallows.

Song birds flit from tree to tree looking for food and filling the forest with their beautiful calls.

High on the wind rides a half dozen vultures, riding the early morning thermals with little effort, while searching the valley floor for a meal.

A bushy-tailed fox squirrel sits poised on a limb near the river, its sharp teeth tearing away at the shell of an acorn, as it turns the nut in its tiny paws. All is serene.

I open my eyes and the beautiful scene from the past fades into the beautiful present. The sun beams down

---

** The design of the Osage village is unclear. Some believe that the huts were grouped together, while others report that there was an elaborate system of separating huts according to groupings; the clans of the sky people on one side, and the earth and water people on the other.

through the trees up on the bluffs, down through the frosty mist that's hanging over the lake on this cold November morning, turning the mist a creamy white.

The sky overhead is a bright blue, streaked only with a few whispy white Cirrus Stratus clouds high above.

Nothing seems to be moving except the ravenous geese, methodically harvesting the succulent foliage. Only an occasional flapping of wings, or a nip at another goose to remind it of its social status in the flock, breaks up the machine-like effect of their feeding.

I quickly return to my coffee pot for a refill, and then back to my vantage point. The mug feels warm in my hands, and the rising steam from the coffee titillates my nose and eyes as I take a sip. Although I feel like taking a walk, I don't want to disturb the tranquility, so I wait.

The Canada Goose, *Branta Canadensis*, is a beautiful creature. Its large streamlined body is colored in grays, browns and white that compliment its neck and head, which are solid black, except for a white stripe that looks like a chin strap or a beard. The goose is a very efficient creature, eating vegetable matter of many kinds, often seen in corn and wheat fields gleaning through the stubble left behind from the fall harvest. They can live on the water as well as the land, and they make the transition from one to the other with little difficulty. Its gracefulness is saved for the water and the sky though.

The long neck of the goose is very beautiful. It allows the bird to raise its head high above the ground, giving it a better view of the area to look for food, or possible predators. Also, it lets the goose reach the leaves of some taller plants, as well as reaching underwater for submerged flora.

It can also be used to send very definite messages to group members. When the neck is held straight out in front of the bird, parallel to the ground, with its beak aimed straight at another goose, or any other transgressor, there's little doubt about its meaning. I've seen geese, dogs, cats, and even people scurry away at the sight of this battering ram coming at them. I stand and watch for a while longer.

Finally the chill wins out and I return to my kitchen for warmth. After eating a hot breakfast, I rebundle and head back outside.

A light breeze has started blowing toward the north, clearing most of the mist from the lake. The sun has started melting much of the frost, leaving the grass saturated with water.

The geese, finally full, move off toward the lake en masse, and I follow. Their earlier quiet feeding is now replaced with loud, raucous honking, their heads held at optimum height, while they waddle off, flapping their huge wings.

The nearly frozen water on the grass quickly soaks through my tennis shoes, leaving my feet wet and cold after just a few steps. I walk across the park lawn despite the cold wet grass, past the handmade wooden play area that attracts dozens of kids on warm afternoons. They play on, around, and under the creative apparatus, exploring all the possibilities of fantasy; turning it into pirate ships, or mountain hide-outs, or hilltop castles, or space ships. But this morning it stands empty and silent.

Reaching the footpath that runs along the lakeshore, I turn northward. The breeze is blowing to my back, so it doesn't feel very cold. As it blows over the top of the lake, it sends miniature waves rippling to the north, and they move along with me.

On the left, at the far edge of the park, where I envisioned the Osage village, is a grove of towering trees. These 50 or so trees are very large, rising well over 150 feet high, and over 15 feet in circumference. Such beautiful creations.

I wonder how long they've stood here, how many times they've played host to birds, and animals, and man, since they first sprouted from the earth.

Their huge size is quite humbling, not unlike standing

next to the giant redwoods in California. Gentle giants.

They stand majestically, like a living altar of creation, reaching toward heaven, but never forgetting to remain a part of the earth. A link between things hoped for and things that are. The breeze rattles the dry leaves that still remain on the high branches.

I walk down the path with the lake on my right and those silent, ominous overlords to my left.

I grew up in a Southern Baptist home in these hills. Religion was a way of life on Sundays and Wednesday night. My mother worked hard to guide the steps of her five natural children and the many more foster children that she's raised.

I never doubted the existence of God, because there wasn't any reason to, and the consequences of doing so were unthinkable to my young mind.

However, many of those hours spent in church were spent in the back pews, or in the balcony, engaged in clandestine games of tic-tac-toe, or drawing pictures of nature scenes. Any diversion to keep from falling victim to boredom.

A part of maturation is the questioning of beliefs and testing foundations for weaknesses. My maturation came, in a sense, much too quickly. At the age of 18, I left these hills to join the military. It was then that the unreality of a distant war quickly became a reality, and many of my previously held beliefs were quickly called into question.

I wasn't in combat, but I was involved in the sending of bombers to the front. However, Larry, the guy I joined with, "bought it" in the 1968 Tet Offensive. He was 19.

There are very few things that I remember specifically about that time, but I do remember where I was when I got the word. My supervisor realized the situation and relieved me from duty for a while. I found a place to be alone and "lost it."

It was then that I began to question the war, my reasons for being a part of the war, my belief in religion, in God, and even in myself. Returning to the Ozarks, I spent many years investigating popular movemments and exotic religions, trying to find answers, but they all seemed to fall short of what I needed.

I moved into the White River region and was surprised to find that there was much more to these hills than I'd realized. This is an incredible place, full of history, diversities and intricacies.

Studying the systems of nature here, I found that they were not only fascinating, but worked very well. They didn't need to be questioned, only understood. And it seems the more I study and learn, the more I seem to know about myself, and find that inner peace that's been so illusive. But I also know that these mountains still have so much to teach me.

The geese have moved up the lake and disappeared from sight. The sun is getting higher, but the cold breeze on my back keeps me from feeling much of its warmth.

All is quiet, except for the breeze blowing through the cottonwood leaves, and the small waves on the lake lapping against the shore.

Here it is November 11, Veterans' Day. A day for remembering those that served so faithfully, and gave their all. I haven't forgotten, and I never will.

Rest in peace, Larry. Rest in peace.

Day Two
December 12

Floods of Emotion

    December days have often been stressful for me. The upcoming holiday triggers many emotions that come from earlier experiences in life. Christmas has never been my favorite time, because I grew up in a family that was financially borderline, and Christmas served to remind me that we didn't have what so many others did. I learned at an early age that wishing and writing letters to Santa Claus were often exercises in futility. All of my hopes and prayers never changed the fact that a twentieth century Christmas is a product of Madison Avenue, for the purpose of generating profits, with little regard for the psychological effects on poor people who are unable to participate.

    As I grew older, my hurt from deprivation changed into hurting for other children who suffer through this period. During this month, I often immerse myself into projects that take most of my time and energies until 12 o'clock midnight, when the date turns to December 26, and all of my dreads mysteriously evaporate.

    Here it is, two weeks before Christmas, and my emotions are in turmoil, but it's not just the season.

    I'm sitting and staring into the swirling waters of Lake Taneycomo as the roar from powerful generators in Table Rock Dam drone on. The mist from the gray sky chills me, but I don't move.

    There is so much in this life that I've yet to understand. The forces that control and fuel this universe are so immense, my mind often seems totally unable to understand the things that are happening. Maybe my mind understands its limits, and refuses to overload itself with incomprehensible data.

    The one area that is hard to understand is death. Is it an end, or a beginning, or merely a continuation? I still do not know.

A few days ago there was stunning news that came from Armenia, one of the many republics that make up the Soviet Union. An earthquake measuring 6.9 on the Richter Scale caused tremendous damage. It wasn't the size of the quake, but the poor building construction that had been the contributing factor.

The loss of life was incredible. Tens of thousands of people were buried alive when the huge stone buildings collapsed.

I felt a strong need to go there and do whatever I could to assist in the relief effort, but as I was making travel plans, a phone call came. There would be no trip to help out in the grief stricken area, because I had my own grief to deal with.

That morning, December 9, two young boys had died in a trailer fire. They were my nephews, ages five and seven. While they slept, dreaming of Santa Claus, their lives ended. The Christmas tree, presents, and the pet dog went with them.

The water in front of me rolls and boils as images play across my mind. Today, at the funeral, I watched my brother as he hugged other people's children, friends of his boys. In his eyes I could see the pain as he wished he could do something, anything to make this nightmare go away. He wanted to wake up and find this only a terrible dream. But this is no dream. There will be no awakening.

I shared tears with a niece, the daughter of a sister, who kept saying, "It's not fair, it's not fair." There was so much I felt I should say, but I didn't know the answer, so the words didn't come.

What is fair? I don't know.

I'm sitting on a large limestone rock, one of thousands of rocks that are piled along the lake bank at the base of Table Rock Dam to keep the churning waters that gush out of the generating turbines from eroding the soil.

The dam looms high to my right, its ten long concrete

spillways looking like drab, gray ski jumps, each arching down from the floodgates, to the cold waters below. The huge, steel floodgates sit on huge tracks which allow them to be raised or lowered, releasing any excess water that's built up on Table Rock Lake. When the gates are opened even a little bit, the water comes cascading down, roaring into Lake Taneycomo below.

A few years ago, when we had had extreme rainfalls, I sat in this very spot watching the watershow as all ten gates were opened one foot. The gates were only left open for one hour because the addition of 26,000 cubic feet of water per second into Taneycomo caused flooding downstream.

This incredible sight is one I'll remember for a long time. Ten identical white waterfalls, racing down the spillways hundreds of feet, crashing with a deafening roar into the frothy waters below.

I think again to the devastation of the Armenian earthquake. What if an earthquake struck here? The largest earthquake in American history struck in December of 1811 just to the east of here at New Madrid, Missouri. It was apparently an unbelievable occurrence. It raised and lowered the earth six to fifteen feet for thousands of miles. And the quaking continued periodically for the next year, with over 2,000 tremors recorded.

I try to imagine what it would be like if we had that kind of earthquake here. It would probably split the dam open, creating a 200 foot wall of water that would wipe out almost everything in its path, all the way to the Mississippi River.

I shudder and my mind blocks out the images as I look up at the huge dam.

This, of course, wouldn't be the first flood down this valley, although it surely would be the worst. Even so, floods have washed these lowlands many times.

The recorded floods happened in 1824, the time when white settlers were first coming into this region, and again in 1844, 1884, 1890, 1927, and 1945. But there is no way of knowing how many times in the past thousands or millions of years that the White River has escaped its banks and ravaged this land. The unrestrained fury of the Ni-U-Skah, La Riviere Blanche, Rio Blanco, White River, and the many forgotten names that came before.

As rain and snow fall on these Ozark Mountains, water runs off the hillsides, down ravenes; emptying into creeks and small rivers, such as Aunt's Creek, Bee Creek, Indian Creek, Long Creek, Fall Creek, Roark Creek, Turkey Creek, Bear Creek, Swan Creek, Beaver Creek, Cedar Creek, and the James River that swell and rush into the White. The voluminous waters overflowing the banks and inundating the river bottoms all along the valley. This water stripping off thousands of tons of topsoil, carrying it along in its muddy deluge.

Very little could stand up to its power. It tore at land, trees, rocks, pulling loose anything that wasn't solidly fastened, dragging it along on its way to the sea.

The flotsam was made up of grasses, sticks, limbs, trees, carcasses, barrels, boxes, wagons, barns, houses, and anything else that would float. Those that wouldn't float were often swept along the bottom by the surging currents.

Each time the flood water receded, it left fields and valleys covered with mud and silt and debris. The branches of bushes and trees were marked by the litter left behind by the flood, showing where the high water had reached.

And, after a time, flood waters would again return to this valley, where the inhabitants could only watch and wonder at the power of the stream as it ran rampant, unchecked, down the valley, leaving another high water mark.

Sometimes the locals would tie a rope to their boat, and the other end to a tree, and paddle out into the raging current to retrieve valuable items as they floated by, and later they would try to return the property to the rightful owners. However, some objects such as houses and barns were just too large to save. The flood waters would carry these treasures off to the east.

But since the construction of Table Rock Dam, this has

all stopped. The million-plus cubic yards of concrete, reinforced with steel and tons and tons of limestone rock that was torn from the side of Baird Mountain, a couple of miles to the east, makes a perfect barrier.

I'm sitting on a large chunk of that rock. Looking down at it, I wonder how many brachiapods, clams, cephlapods, and snails it took to form this one rock. And what of the thousands and millions of other rocks that surround this spillway, and help make up the causeway, and that were used in the construction of the 252 foot high, 1,602 foot long dam itself.

It took millions of years of tides, rising and falling in the several seas that have inundated this land. The many storms, and waves, and unseen currents that carried species after species along their individual evolutionary paths. And how many unknown types of animals are also buried in this rock. Life, and then death. All that remains are the minerals that they left behind, their usefulness unknown. Their adaptability not keeping up with the changing order of things, becoming extinct; as every known kind of life probably will eventually be, left behind as nature ever changes, ever creating new species, more adaptable to an ever changing world.

My thoughts are interupted by a small group of starlings that alight in an elm tree off to the left. They hold tightly, keeping their balance, as the branches swing back and forth.

The starling, *starnus vulgaris vulgaris*, is a perfect example of man's continual intrusion into the natural order of things. Originally a European bird, they were introduced to America in 1890, when 60 starlings were released in Central Park in New York City. The following year, 40 more were released. The starlings, which are strongly adaptable, and are also fairly aggressive, flourished. From those original 100 birds, millions now range over much of the United States and parts of Canada. Being quite competitive, they have taken over many of the home ranges of native song birds.

Although their introduction hasn't brought the devastation that the introduction of rabbits did to Australia, or the brown tree snake did on Guam, still the starling has had a major impact on American wildlife, and will continue to unless nature is allowed to create a balance by increasing the numbers of predators.

Two of the starlings fly down to the lake's edge for a drink, and then begin to scour the ground for food. Their quick, nervous, erratic walk makes them easily distinguishable from the common blackbirds and grackles that often travel with them in mixed flocks. Even though the starling is not a popular bird, it does have several beautiful calls, often mimicking other birds.

I watch the birds in the tree jumping from limb to limb, carrying on an excited conversation. I'm not sure what it is they're discussing. It might be me, or a cat lurking close by, or the colder weather that's moving in.

The birds that were on the ground fly back up with the others. Watching them interact, I try to imagine how they've changed over the last few million years. These small, singing animals that can travel great distances with seemingly little effort are much older than they appear. It is believed that these small feathered creatures are not distant relatives of, but rather direct descendants of the great dinosaurs.

The skeletal structure of a bird's head is very much like that of the Truladon, which was a close relative of Tyrannosaurus Rex, the fiercest dinosaur known. I look hard to see a connection, but of course, 150 million years of evolution can make a great deal of difference.

These small creatures certainly must have a great ability to adapt, because they are still here. Their larger relatives died out during the cretaceous period, about 65 million years ago; the reason unknown. It may have been a virus, or a sudden change in the climate, or as one theory has it, a large meteorite may have struck the earth, creating a firestorm. This was followed by year around winter caused by thick clouds of smoke that kept the sun's rays from entering the atmosphere. This is the same scenario of what might happen in the event of a nuclear war.

The dinosaurs are gone, but left behind are the birds. I still have trouble seeing the connection. When I look at elephants, rhinocerouses, alligators and crocodiles, lizards, turtles, etc., the similarities are evident, but these birds are different. It must be the feathers. There are no pictures of dinosaurs with feathers. A bird or chicken or turkey without feathers is a very strange looking creature indeed. Not totally unlike drawings I've seen of Tyrannosaurus Rex and his relatives. But wouldn't it be ironic if some of the drawings were wrong? What if some of the dinosaurs had feathers, or were at least much hairier than we believe? Who knows?

Across the lake, flying in short spurts, goes a red-bellied woodpecker, *melanerpes carolinas*. It is also called the zebra woodpecker, because of the black and white markings on its back and wings, as well as being known as the sapsucker or chamchak. It seems odd that it is called red-bellied though, since the red is on its head and sometimes the nape of the neck, but its underside is mostly white. It flies along, obviously unconcerned with what it's called.

It lands on the side of a large oak tree, and quickly works its way around the trunk to the other side, disappearing from view. In a few minutes it reappears, intently searching the tree's surface for anything edible. With a sudden burst, it flits off into the trees, out of sight.

The starlings are still chattering in the elm, but my gaze goes back to the water. So much power, swirling, rolling. The rise and fall of the boiling water gives me a feeling of vertigo, not unlike the sensation I used to have as a child lying in bed at night with my eyes closed, letting my thoughts fly free. It was then that I saw a gray cloud in my mind that seemed to flow over me, pulling me ever deeper into its void, until I would shutter and block it from my mind. Fear of the unknown. I've often wondered if it was death or deathlike.

The water surges on.

When the four generators of this dam are turned on, they can each produce 50,000 kilowatts of electricity per hour, as one and a half million gallons of water per minute pass through the turbines of each generator. All four generators can expel 360 million gallons per hour, which is enough water to totally replace the water in Lake Taneycomo in a 24-hour period.

That's the reason that when Table Rock Dam went on-line in 1959, the temperature of Lake Taneycomo dropped rapidly, and changed this boating and recreational lake into a trout fishing lake. Resort areas on Taneycomo, such as Rockaway Beach, were greatly affected, as boaters and skiers moved to the other side of Table Rock Dam to enjoy the warmer water on top of Table Rock Lake.

I think again to the immense force that's stored high above me to my right. Poised, ominous, still. The billions of gallons of water in the 43,000 acre lake, held back by one and one quarter million cubic yards of concrete adjoining the three and one third million cubic yards of earth embankment.

The pressure at the bottom of the lake at the base of the dam is tremendous. If I were an eighth of a mile to my right, I would have thousands of pounds of additional weight pushing down on me from the water above. The dark cloud would again come rolling over me, pulling me into its void.

The milky green, oxygen-laden water continues to roll by, foaming slightly as trapped bubbles of air fight to escape. A cold mist rides along above the water, following it downstream; radiation fog.

My thoughts backtrack a few weeks to Thanksgiving day. The turkey and dressing sitting on the table, along with green beans, corn, mashed potatoes and gravy, casseroles, homemade breads, and several pies and cakes.

Part of the family had made it to Mom and Dad's, and three grandkids and two foster kids ran through the house to keep things from becoming too peaceful. They would run out the front door, slamming it behind them, or leaving it ajar as they hurried out to play in the yard, or on the surrounding hills. And then, as quickly as they had left, they would run back in, tracking mud with them. They were too excited to eat anything but the sweets. A piece of pumpkin pie or peanut bread crammed into little mouths with hands dirty from playing, as they hurried back outside. Their hair matted by sweat, shirt tails hanging out, pant knees covered with mud, their cheeks flushed, and their noses running. Each moment lived to the fullest. No tomorrows, only now.

These memories are all that remain of the two of them. What's happened since that day seems so unreal. I can't deny that they are gone, but I also can't fully accept it either. That's a part of life that is so difficult, the passing of someone you know, especially ones that are so young.

I want to believe that death isn't some dark spirit that is waiting to rob us of life. I want to understand just what it is, or isn't, whether it is another plane of existence or a state of non-life. I don't know, and so I'm filled with a fear of the unknown, the misunderstood, and all those fears as a child come creeping back. I feel the dark cloud rolling over me as I fear the thing we call death.

I've read many books on different concepts about death. Heaven, nirvana, reincarnation, the one, the void; nothingness. So many people claim to know, but none have been there. At least, not the ones that talk to me. I've always been reluctant to follow or believe self-proclaimed experts who haven't done something themselves. I'm a skeptic.

But I'm also hopeful. I want to believe that in these churning waters, or this chilly December air, or in the gray cloudy sky, there is an answer. Maybe these hills will reveal it to me, or maybe they already have and I have yet to understand the message. It might be buried in this rock I'm sitting on, buried with the countless creatures that are now a part of it.

The bluff across the lake rises over 200 feet straight up. Maybe somewhere in the strata, buried for millions of years is the clue that will unlock the mystery. One thing is for certain: I will know, or not know, which will negate my questions anyway, at the moment I too reach that point in my life when the dark cloud descends completely; the end.

The end. How final it sounds. How absolute. I wonder how many living organisms have reached the end. Lived and then died. The numbers are far beyond my comprehension. The end was reached by the billions of animals it took to make up these rocks. And the countless microscopic marine animals that helped make up, but are now only elemental parts of, the passing water. Everything living, and then dying.

The starlings don't seem to care. They have all flown to the ground and are scurrying about, looking for food. Step, step, step, step, peck. They seem to know that if they don't get enough to eat, they'll understand "the end" all too well. Step, step, step, step, peck.

Sometimes it seems it would be easier to be a bird. The seasons would control your life. There would be a time for building, mating, parenthood. A time for storing up fat reserves. A time for migrating. No close ties, no need for any ideology. No funerals or unanswered questions about life and death. Only living. Perch in a tree and sleep. Wake up and call and feed. And the seasons would tell you when to do each. No trying to control the world with machines, or trying to change it to fit your needs, but fitting into the world as it is. Accepting the floods as they come, not needing to build huge dams to block the earth's arteries. And accepting death by living. Step, step, step, step, peck.

I am amazed at the adaptability of the creatures of this world, and how, when they no longer can adapt to the changes, they reach the end, the place I fear.

But why do I fear it so? It is inevitable. 99.9% of all species that have lived here are now extinct. All of their family members are dead. Man, too, is but a momentary visitor in this world, so he, too, must pass on. Someday mankind will be just another extinct species. I won't be alone in death. But still...

I lay back on the rocks and look up into the gray, hazy sky. There's not much to see except on occasional sparrow or starling passing overhead. A fleeting image.

The American flag atop the dam is standing straight out in the strong wind that blows off of Table Rock Lake, but here on the dam's lee side I'm sheltered from the harsh wind. But still it's cold.

High up on the bluff across from me is a scenic view area. I watch as a family gets out of their car and walks up to chain link fence that keeps sightseers away from the dangerous cliff's edge. From their vantage point the family can look down on the ten concrete spillways that arch down to the churning waters below. They can look north and east across the surrounding hills of oak, hickory, and cedar that are dotted with homes, summer cabins, and trailers.

Down to their right, my left, they can see the 24 rectangular concrete lagoons that are used at the hatchery to raise the hundreds of thousands of baby trout that will someday swim free in Lake Taneycomo and area streams. The lagoons also offer a veritable feast for an opportunistic bald eagle that might chance by.

The family stands and points off in different directions. The man is taking pictures of the scenery.

Two small children go running along the fence toward the dam. The smaller one in front must be about four or five. Running, running.

I close my eyes and see other children running. Running in the door, grabbing pumpkin pie and peanut bread, cramming it into their mouths with dirty hands, hair matted with sweat, shirt tails hanging out, pants streaked with mud, and then running back out the door, slamming it behind them. Cheeks flushed, noses running.

I look again at the churning, rolling water. It boils and tumbles as the generators drone on. Everything around me turns gray and misty.

I sit alone on the rocks and cry.

Day Three
January 19

Meeting on the Hill

    The cold January air burns my nose as I make my way up the north slope of Snapp Bald. This hill is made up of mostly rock, covered with a layer of soil that supports an assortment of grasses, composites, and scraggly trees, mostly cedar.
    Here on the shaded north side of the hill, moss and lichens cover most of the ground and exposed slabs of rock. The moisture in and underneath the moss has frozen into minute crystal formations, which makes an exaggerated crunching sound as they shatter under my feet. It sounds something like walking on piles of egg shells.
    Clumps of scruffy looking red cedar trees are scattered about the hill. The greener colored females are covered with small, chalky blue berries, while the more reddish colored males stand barren.
    Occasionally hidden among the cedars is an undernourished elm, oak, sumac or catalpa tree. The trees stand in sharp contrast to the tawny tufts of broom sedge that wave in the cold northwest wind; the two-foot stems of the sedge having dried and the seed pods splitting open to expose tiny seeds with their feathery plumes. Now the seeds wave in the wind, waiting to be knocked loose by a passing animal or the wind or the rain.
    The afternoon sun makes these tiny seeds look even more delicate, but I'm sure they are quite resilient as they patiently await the passing of winter on this hill.
    Snapp Bald, Old Bald, Bald Knob; these are some of the names given to this hill back in the 1880's when it apparently didn't have any trees on it.
    Walking to the top, I can see buildings ten miles to the west, out beyond Branson, southward as far as the Arkansas state line, northward to an old rock quarry and the

ridge that Highway 160 runs along, and off to the east I can see Forsyth and the hills that lie far beyond that near Hercules Glades. If the cedar trees weren't here, my view of the surrounding area would be totally unobstructed. The men that came to this hill in January, 1885 ,knew what they were doing.

The Ozarks region at that time was still rebuilding after the Civil War. These hill people, some who had been here since white men first settled in this region in the 1820's, and others who had moved here after the war, wanted a place they could peacefully raise their families.

The need for law and order is always primary for a civilized society, and the Ozarks was in great need since it was still a wild frontier.

During the war there had been a homeguard established to fight against the outlaws and ruffians that terrorized the citizens. But the homeguard was usually called upon only after someone had been victimized.

One such episode took place after bushwhackers hanged the elderly father of a homeguard leader, when the old man refused to disclose his hidden money. The guard was quickly called out and gave chase. They caught up with the outlaws between Reeds Spring and Galena, killing several of the desperados, leaving their bodies by a pond for the scavengers.

Another bushwhacker who had terrorized the area during the war moved back into the area to live. The homeguard pulled him from his cabin and took him to Devil's Den (now known as Marvel Cave, which lies underneath Silver Dollar City, west of Branson), and threw him from the opening at the top into the 200 foot deep main room. Both the pond and the cave were later thought to be haunted by the men's ghosts and were avoided.

But even with the avenging homeguard, lawlessness was rampant. The terrain and location of the Ozarks made it easy for someone to break the law, then hide out or slip into Arkansas or Oklahoma to avoid punishment.

Also, there were many close-knit family groups that protected the interest of wayward family members. Even if the offender was arrested and brought to trial, often the jury, being made up of family and friends, would set the culprit free.

During the period between the Civil War and 1885, there were over thirty unsolved, unprosecuted murders in Taney County alone. And there were bullies and rabble-rousers that ran roughshod over the community.

Some of the citizens grew outraged by the lack of law and decided to establish their own police force. Eleven men met in the back room of a store in Forsyth to lay the groundwork for the organization, and then put out a notice for an open meeting.

The exact date of the first open meeting is not certain. Some reports show it to be April, but others claim it was January. Regardless, I'm now standing on the summit of the hill where the self-appointed leaders met with their supporters.

It gives me an unexplainable feeling to visit different historical sites, many of which are unmarked and unnoticed by most people, but the happenings at that location had a profound influence on the history of the Ozarks. As I stand here, I realize that time alone keeps me from witnessing the meeting.

I recall a movie about a time machine and wish that I had such a vehicle, enabling me to witness all the history of these hills, much of which is lost forever, and I could see for myself if the verbal accounts of that first meeting were correct, that this hill was "black with men." Maybe it is true.

But now, I stand alone, except for the patches of rust tinted red cedar trees, on top of this tall, rounded knob, covered with dried broom sedge, with the bright blue January sky all around, the cold northwest wind blowing past me with little effect. Here at the top, the thin, rocky soil of the surrounding hill has given way, exposing large slabs of bare, weathered limestone rock. It's a solid place to stand and view my world.

Ten decades ago these same rocks held groups of roughly dressed mountain men, dressed in homespun wools, tanned leathers, and hats of furs and felt, many armed with pistols, shotguns, squirrel guns, and razor sharp knives, their well-worn, roughly cobbled shoes and boots shuffled about on these limestone slabs, while they listened and talked with their leaders.

Down below, their horses and mules, some without saddles or leather bridles, were tethered to bushes or hobbled in the open. There, where the animals contented themselves with the dried grasses, guards were posted to meet the new arrivals. The muffled sounds of their voices seem to still hang in the timeless air. According to the book, *The Baldknobbers*, by Lucille Morris Upton, the code went like this:

"Boy, she pops," began the code.
"Who goes there?"
"Bell."
"Whose bell?"
"My bell," or "Your bell."

With the proper passwords being exchanged, another would join the meeting on the hill.

One of the founding fathers, Captain Nat. N. Kinney, his 6'7", 275 pound frame, complete with his side gun, undoubtedly looked formidable standing here on top of Snapp Bald.

This spot is just south of the Oak Grove School that Captain Kinney was instrumental in building. The one room, stone schoolhouse still stands, with its high, windowless west wall, and its eastern wall, replete with windows. These windows may have been added later, since glass for windows was still a rare commodity here in the 1880's.

But here, on Snapp Bald, there is nothing to mark this site as the meeting place of the Baldknobbers.

The group itself didn't choose the Baldknobber name for it's organization, but others began calling them by that name since they met on a bald knob.

The objectives that they established were not only to fight against lawlessness that ranged from murder to stealing, but to police moral improprieties, such as moonshining, wife beating, and drunkeness.

This group was not unlike the many other vigilante organizations that have cropped up when people feel that their lives and lifestyles are threatened. The Ku Klux Klan was in full swing farther south, being organized after the Civil War to fight the perceived threat of recently freed slaves that were exercising their rights at the expense of the Southern status quo, and also the influx of northern carpetbaggers who saw the economically devastated south as "ripe for the picking."

No matter what the initial purposes of these organizations, without an internal policing policy, they become more and more subjective in their interpretation of right and wrong, and the means by which they can achieve justice, often, in the end, becomes a greater threat to society than the one they are fighting.

Captain Kinney, although obviously a charismatic leader, would have been a perfect candidate for an intense background investigation had he lived today.

He claimed he was a captain in the Union Army during the war, but some reports say he was only a private. After the war he worked as a special agent for the Post Office, and wasn't opposed to using his gun. He killed several people he claimed resisted arrest. He also worked as a detective for the railroad. He'd been a tavern owner in Springfield, which had made him the money to retire in these Ozark mountains. But after he arrived with his family, and their expensive furniture, part of which was the only piano in the White River area, he quickly established himself, with the help of his friend Alonzo Prather, retired State Representative, who lived in Kirbyville, as a strong civic leader.

This area, with its ever present problems with lawlessness, was a perfect setting for a citizens' group to form.

Farmers were reporting that their cattle were being mutilated, a problem that reoccurs periodically even today. And after a storekeeper in Forsyth was shot and killed, and the killer tried and released, the Baldknobbers organized.

One of their policing procedures was to place a bundle of switches on the porch of a wrong-doer. That meant straighten up, or else. However, if the warning was not heeded, the stubborn offender would be dragged out and beaten.

At first the Baldknobbers wore handkerchiefs and other disguises, but a more standard uniform evolved. It consisted of black or dark gray feed sacks worn over their heads. The upper corners of the sack were tied with red strings, making them look like horns with red tassles hanging off. Holes were cut for the eyes and mouth and those were circled with white paint. They also covered their shoes and boots with socks, making identification more difficult.

But since there weren't many people living in Taney County, the offender knew that these were his neighbors. This added to the intimidation, and to the opposition of the Baldknobbers, since many of these hill folks were fiercely independent and defied anyone who tried to tell them what to do.

The group continued to grow stronger and bolder, exercising its full power with the Taylor boys. They were local ruffians that terrorized an elderly couple from England, the Dickensons, who had a store five miles north of Forsyth at a place called Taney City. They shot the couple and left them for dead, but the couple survived.

The Taylors hid out, but when they found out that the elderly couple hadn't died, they turned themselves into the authorities to avoid being found by the Baldknobbers who were searching for them.

At nightfall, one hundred Baldknobbers rode into Forsyth, closing off the streets. They went to the unguarded jailhouse and broke down the door with sledgehammers. They took the screaming brothers, Frank and Tubal, to a place north of Forsyth where they tried, convicted and hanged them, and left them hanging for others to see. Their judgment was quick and final.

In a lot of ways, this form of justice is appealing. There was no need for public defenders, or batteries of lawyers, no pyschiatric evaluations, countless legal briefs, motions and appeals. The legal process wasn't drawn out for months, years, ad infinitum.

The Dickensons were not subjected to barrages of slurs and innuendos by Machiavellian lawyers who often forget who is the victim and who is the victimizer. There were no wasted tax dollars, nor handcuffing of the legal system, as appeal after appeal, and stay after stay, filled the court dockets. They were tried, convicted, and hanged, in a few minutes of time.

Although this appears to have been an efficient form of the judicial process, it was wide open for extreme abuses.

Politics undoubtedly entered into the judgments handed down, or not handed down, to lawbreakers. It is believed that almost all of the Baldknobbers belonged to one political party, and most of their opposition was on the other side.

There was a growing resentment to the Baldknobbers. The anti-Baldknobbers, many of whom had undoubtedly run up against the night riders, but also others who merely saw them as terrorists rather than public protectors, tried to sway public opinion.

And sometimes, showing disrespect for the group could prove nearly fatal. One farmer who came too close to a Baldknobber meeting showed a lack of discretion by verbally antagonizing them. To teach him a lesson, they hanged him up with bridle lines around his head. They had only meant to scare him, but he passed out, barely escaping serious injury. This further fed the flames of resistance to the self-styled police force.

The anti-Baldknobbers, also known as "Slickers," stepped up their opposition.

On a Sunday in March 1886, a young tough by the name of Andrew Cogburn, undoubtedly to gain a reputation, confronted Captain Kinney at the Oak Grove Church, just before evening services. Cogburn had apparently been bragging that he was going to kill Kinney. Kinney was carrying a warrant for Cogburn's arrest that a deputy sheriff had asked Kinney to serve.

By most accounts, Cogburn came around the church, gun in hand. Kinney reportedly tried to arrest Cogburn, who raised his gun at Kinney. Kinney drew and fired, killing Cogburn.

Sam Snapp, a friend of Cogburn's who was the only non-Baldknobber witness, disappeared for a time, so the only witnesses to the shooting were Baldknobbers. Kinney was exonerated.

This incident sent the anti-Baldknobbers representatives to the state capitol to ask Governor Marmaduke to send a militia force to fight the Baldknobbers. The governor refused.

The Baldknobbers themselves chose to meet with a representative of the governor who'd been sent to Forsyth. The representative stated he didn't disagree with their objectives, but informed them that the formation of such a vigilante group was illegal. The five hundred Baldknobbers that were at that April meeting agreed and pledged to disband.

Although many claim they kept their pledge to ride no more, there still were switches left during the night, and wrong-doers being flogged. These later actions were blamed on imposters who enjoyed the power associated with the Balknobber name.

A month after the group disbanded, Sam Snapp got into

a fight with a friend of Captain Kinney, Wash Middleton, who shot Snapp three times, killing him.

Since public opinion was turning against the Baldknobbers, Middleton was tried and sentenced to forty years in the penitentiary. This was reduced to fifteen years, but in early 1887, he escaped the Forsyth jail, and was never recaptured. It's believed he went to Arkansas.

There was another hanging that took place in Taney County in 1892, but that wasn't attributed to the Baldknobbers, but rather to outraged citizens who hanged a man for brutally killing his wife and leaving her body for the hogs.

The Baldknobber organization in Christian County, however, didn't disband. They continued their night rides until a fateful night near "Smelter Holler" in March of 1887.

They had only planned on getting together and destroying a whiskey still, but some bad blood between the Baldknobbers and a family named Edens that lived along the way, changed that. They decided to stop off and teach them a lesson. The situation quickly got out of hand with William Edens and his brother-in-law, Charles Green, being killed.

That incident led to the end of the Baldknobber era in the Ozarks, and began one of the most publicized trials.

I again look down at the bare slabs of limestone. These rocks were formed about 280 million years ago during the Mississippian period, one of the several times this land was under the sea. These seas teemed with brachiopods, clams, cephlopods, and snails. Their skeletons built up for five million years to form this limestone. How strange that at another time I would be standing at the bottom of a sea, but now I'm standing on top of an Ozark mountain called Snapp Bald.

It's also ironic that this hill where the Baldknobbers first met carries the same name as the man who lost his life for being an enemy of the Baldknobbers, Sam Snapp.

The afternoon sun is beginning to cast long shadows

across the hill. The yellow sunlight washes over the stalks of broom sedge, turning them a bright gold.

As I stand in the shadow of a cedar, a Northern Harrier, *circus cyaneus*, passes a few feet over my head, flying into the northwest wind with no notice of me. I turn and watch as it glides down toward the valley below.

Turning toward the east I see the first signs of the waxing moon as it shows itself over the distant hills far beyond Forsyth. There are still a couple of days before it is full, but it will still give off enough light for a good night of coon hunting. A hunter's moon.

Raccoon hunting is an age-old sport in these hills. It not only offers a way to make some money by selling the hides, but it's also a perfect excuse to get out of the house and enjoy the out of doors.

In these hills, raccoon hunting is serious business. In days gone by, any old "pot licker" would do, but now coon dogs of the highest pedigree are raised for hunting. A good Blue Tick, Black and Tan, or a Walker can bring a hefty price, some costing anywhere from a few dollars to several thousand dollars. Some hunters have been accused of caring more for their dogs than for their families.

Occasionally a hunter will spend days driving along back roads, knocking on farmhouse doors, trying to locate a lost dog. Ads in local newspapers and calls to radio shows are also common.

Tonight the baying of hounds will undoubtedly echo through the valleys as they chase their quarry. And as they run through the fields and forests, the answering barks of watchdogs responding to the commotion cause residents to peer out their windows into the darkness. But the hounds are unconcerned with anything except the hunt.

But what about the raccoon, *procyon lotor*, lotor being a Latin word meaning washer. This, of course, is a misunderstanding of the animal's eating habits. I remember as a kid being told that these animals were very clean, because they constantly washed their food. Later, I discovered that this distant relative of the Asian panda has to wet its food because it doesn't salivate properly. Often the picture of these masked creatures is one of them constantly dipping their food into the water, using their tiny hands. The Indians observed this and named them "Arakunem," hand scratcher.

But this cute, ring tailed animal can also be a very fierce adversary. Many an inexperienced dog has lost its life, or been severely injured, because it underestimated a coon. That's why several dogs are used in the chase on these cold winter nights.

The coon hunters seems little affected by the cold and they say, "The colder, the better." That's because the raccoon pelts are of better quality and don't lose as much hair in colder weather.

The hunt usually starts in the evening when the hunters turn their dogs loose to run the open timberland, trying to locate a fresh scent. And once they find it, the chase may end quickly, or may go on for hours, ending only when the dogs lose the scent or the raccoon takes refuge in a tree.

Hunters become so familiar with their dogs, they can identify each one by its individual bark. When the raccoon is treed, the baying takes on a different sound, signalling the hunters to move in.

The raccoons are usually taken with a small caliber rifle, so that minimal damage is done to the pelt. The skins are often used commercially in the trimming of clothes, and are sometimes labeled as Alaskan sable or Alaskan bear.

The prices for the pelts vary, due to the quality and availability. Sizes also vary because raccoons can weigh anywhere from fifteen to fifty pounds each.

Some coon hunters travel on foot, but others prefer to ride mules. Mules aren't as comfortable to ride as horses, but they are more sure footed. This animal, which is Missouri's mascot, is a usually sterile hybrid that comes from the crossing of a male donkey and a female horse. Raising mules is still a proud profession in these hills.

Looking across the mountains to the east, I wonder how many such night hunts have taken place in these Ozarks. The melodious chorus of running hounds, chasing their frightened, elusive quarry. The hunters sitting around an open campfire, listening to its hissing and crackling wood, watching smoke trail upward, carrying sparks up into the cold January night, often sharing a jar of homebrew to numb their senes to the bitter cold. They swap stories and listen to their dogs sounding over the hills and down the canyons, mixed in with the calls of night birds and the frantic yapping of coyotes preparing for their own night hunt. Shadowy night creatures move secretively through the forest.

It's understandable why some people would prefer this setting to the more confining hearth and home, and civilization.

Here I stand on this isolated bald, the northwest wind to my back, the golden setting sun reflecting off the waving strands of broom sedge. The dried remains of wild licorice, goldenrod, grayhead cornflowers, and tickle grass rustle in the wind.

The rock slabs are solid and unmoving beneath my feet. In the east the moon is rising above the land.

In the movies, this is where the story would end. The setting is peaceful, and the sun is setting. But in these hills, there is no ending, because all stories are continued, sequel after sequel, a series. One chapter ending while another begins.

In these forests that ever sprout, grow, die, and sprout again, it never ends. The harrier flies for a while, and then falls, but another takes its place.

The raccoon lives its nine or ten years, if not caught in a night hunt. Each year the female gives birth to four or five offspring that will join the cycle.

The Baldknobbers, the citizens of these hills that banded together for what they saw as a public good, are also gone. Some are buried at Kirbyville, or the old Wright Cemetery near the Oak Grove School, or elsewhere. But their descendants live on.

Traveling down Ozark roads, I see mailboxes and businesses that bear familiar names, such as Kinney, Fickle, Everett, Rice, Phillips, Van Zandt, Brown, Branson, McHaffie, Delong, and the names of those that ran up against the Baldknobbers, like Snapp, Layton, Greene, Edens, and Taylor. Some of these names are directly tied to the rich history of these hills.

I am a first generation "hillbilly," although my dad has lived most of his life here. My mom came from the Boston Mountains in Arkansas as a young woman, where she met and married my dad. These Ozarks are home, and I'm proud to be a part of them.

As I stand here on this hill, only time separates me from those who took part in those earlier meetings. Looking out across the same hills they scanned, and standing on the same limestone slabs that the captain and his followers stood on, I get a feeling of comradeship.

And tonight, when the moonlight shines down on cedar flocked hilltops, and casts its shadows through the lowland forests of oak, hickory, gum, maple, sycamore, chinquapin, blackjack, and pine, and its ghostly light turns the golden broom sedge to a soft silver, and as the coon dogs run, their bays echoing through the woods and river bottoms, I'll be there, listening, feeling the chase, smelling the campfire smoke as it rises toward the stars, and feeling the fresh, cold night air on my face and ears. Because the more I learn about this land, not only do I become a part of it, but increasingly, it becomes a part of me.

Day Four
February 18

Resourceful Land

I wake up to a world of white. Four inches of soft snow covers the ground outside, while large, feathery flakes continue to fall. Tree limbs and bushes become bowed under the growing weight of the snow as it accumulates.

Occasionally a pile of snow breaks free of its limb support and crashes to the ground with a thud, trailing a stream of snow particles behind; a miniature comet.

I raise a window to get a better view, and cold air rushes in. It smells clean and fresh. The crisp sleet-like sound of snow flakes striking frozen limbs is the only sound.

Snow is not unknown in the Ozarks, but still we only get about two or three measurable amounts annually, with a total accumulation between five and eighteen inches. Even so, these smaller amounts make getting up and down these hills difficult, so this snow will undoubtedly cause some inconvenience. However, I plan on enjoying it.

I fix a quick breakfast and down my morning coffee. A quick shower, and then I start bundling up for a sojourn into the cold.

Slipping on my insulated underwear and then covering them with two more layers of clothing, I discover just how restricting clothes can be as I try to lace up my boots. It takes longer than I had planned.

After slipping on my coat, ski mask, and gloves, I step out, hearing a crunch as my feet hit the snow.

The world is so beautiful.

The sound of the falling flakes is much louder now as they hit the limbs and also fall against my nylon coat. The sound is constant, but not oppressive.

Now and then a flake catches on one of my eyelashes that protrude from the eye holes in my mask. Blinking my eyes, I feel the cold of the melting flake as it falls on my upper cheek. A few more steps and my lashes catch another flake.

All is peaceful.

Walking along, I notice a unique sound coming from each step. As my body weight passes from heel to toe, snow is compressed under my foot, resisting, until most of my weight is on my toes, when there comes a muffled pop, as the snow surrenders, but not without a noise of protest. Each step sounds the same; crunch, pop. Crunch, pop. Crunch, pop.

The dark trunked trees, their forks, limb tops, and windward sides painted with swatches of white, stand out in the bright world all around them.

The dead leaves and fallen branches that cover the ground are hidden under the blanket of white. Only an occasional bump or mound hints at the disguised presence of a clump of grass, a rock, a stick or a stump.

This early in the morning, I've beaten most creatures out into the new snow, so there is little disturbance of the uniform whiteness. That is, until I look behind me and see my winding, uneven tracks despoiling the scene.

At first I walk with no particular destination in mind, since I just enjoy looking at the even layer of snow everywhere that hides holes, ditches, and obstacles. The roofs of houses and sheds are covered with the same soft snow. At the edges of the roofs hang different sized icicles where water started to drip, and froze before it could fall, building downward, drop after drop. Icy stalactites.

The heavily flocked limbs of red cedar trees and a solitary lilac bush bend toward the ground.

Coming to a place that opens into a field, I misjudge where the ditch is hiding, and step off into a twelve inch drift, stumbling, and nearly falling on my face.

The field resembles a miniature mountain range, as clumps of grass are covered to look like mountain peaks. Only the occasional stem of a foxtail, or an unrelinquishing strand of johnson grass stands above the scene, destroying the effect.

As I walk through the open field, I come across a set of tracks, the first I've seen. The two, long parallel marks, followed by a single, small round mark, are obviously the footprints of a cottontail rabbit, *sylvilagus*. Rabbits are prolific rodents that seems to adapt well to almost every climate. When European rabbits were introduced to Australia, they didn't have any natural enemies there, and began reproducing wildly, quickly reaching pandemic proportions. It was only after the Australians introduced the rabbit disease myxomatosis, in 1950, that the rabbits were somewhat controlled.

Here in the Ozarks, however, the rabbit has many enemies that work well to keep it in check. Not only do foxes, coyotes, hawks, owls, eagles, bobcats, dogs, and house cats count it as prey, but man has also added many a rabbit to his cooking pot, despite the fact that the wild rabbit sometimes carries the infectious disease tularemia, rabbit fever, which can be transmitted to man.

In these hills, rabbits are frequently hunted, and snowy days like this make the hunting easier, since their tracks give them away.

A stick poked into one of those snowy covered grass clumps or used to beat on a brush pile will often prove fruitful, as a brown, furry flash explodes from its hiding place.

If the snow is exceptionally deep, eight or more inches, rabbits can actually be caught by hand, since they aren't equipped like their cousin, the snowshoe rabbit, and their smaller feet break through the snow's surface. The cottontails flounder, and have to jump higher to clear the snow, slowing them down.

Even so, most hunting is done with guns, and is aided by the use of dogs, usually beagles, that are trained to chase the rabbit in a large circle, bringing it back around toward the hunter. Most rabbits are taken with a small shotgun or a .22 caliber rifle.

Growing up, I remember hunting these animals with rocks, sticks, and even railroad spikes that were discarded by a nearby railway.

My older brother took hunting to greater degrees. He built a rabbit trap, a long, rectangular, wooden box with a sliding door that would slide shut once the rabbit, or whatever, touched the baited triggering device on the inside. The animal would be captured alive and unharmed.

This made retrieving the catch a bit risky, since the animal on the inside couldn't be seen until the box was opened. Occasionally skunks, opossums or raccoons went for the bait. Luckily, my brother never met up with the wrong end of a skunk, requiring a great deal of isolation, and baths in tomato juice.

He also became enamored with trapping, acquiring a few small steel leg traps that he placed along a nearby stream. His success was minimal though.

I don't really enjoy hunting or trapping, but both activities have great significance in these hills, since they were important industries here. The first white men who came into this region, besides those doing mineral exploration, were looking for furs.

The Ozarks have supported an abundance of fur bearing animals, such as squirrels, rabbits, beaver, mink, weasel, fox, opossum, raccoon, muskrat, skunk, coyote, bobcat, deer, along with the now absent bison, elk, black bear, panther, antelope, badger, otter and wolf. I again wish that time would give me a chance to go back and see these hills as they were.

I did see a panther on a couple of occasions a few summers ago, but it must have been migrating through here. I would like to see it again, or see a wolf on a hunt, or a herd of buffalo contentedly chewing cud, or a majestic bull elk trumpeting his high pitched call in the excitement of rut, or the powerful black bear.

The bear has always been a fascinating animal. Since it's an omnivour, with 90% of its food coming from vegetation, the Indians saw it as more human than animal. It would disappear for six months, and then reappear with fully developed young in the spring. It was looked upon as the great Earth Mother, a god-like spirit come to earth. The Indians hoped to draw powers from it by wearing bear skin robes, complete with head and claws, and calling themselves the Bear Clan.

I'd love to watch bears in these forests, as they feed day and night, sleeping little, consuming their 20,000 calories a day, building up their four inches of fat, and three more inches of fur. Constantly roaming, nibbling, sniffing, digging, fishing, and eating.

But now, in this cold February whiteness, even if the black bear did still roam these hills, it would be hidden underground in a cave or hollow, its heart beating ten times a minute, its stomach and intestines completely shut down; no eating or excreting for six months. Cubs being born while the mothers sleep, unaware. Special hormones in its system retrieving calcium and phosphorous lost when bones atrophy during non-use, and the waste urea, a by-product of the digestion of fats and proteins, magically turned back into amino acids and complex proteins by a still mysterious process in the bear's kidneys and liver.

But trappers and hunters didn't care about the mysteries of the bear or panther or beaver. All that was important was the pelt. A pelt was as good as gold.

Small steamboats would come up on the White River from Batesville, Arkansas, trading molasses and sugar brought from New Orleans for furs and hides.

There were three large fur companies based in St Louis: The Missouri Fur Trading Company, The Rocky Mountain Fur Company, and The American Fur Trading Company. And with these companies needing furs, fur trapping in this region flourished.

But furs weren't the only offerings here. This area hosted passenger pigeons, eskimo curlew, Louisiana parquets, ivory-billed woodpeckers, whistling swans, all of which are no longer here. However, there is still the wild turkey, bobwhite quail, mourning dove, mallard, blue-winged teal, wood duck, and Canadian geese, among others, that live in the fields and forests and streams.

And the streams offer even more. Fishing has always been a staple for man in this region, since the earliest Paleo-Indians arrived here around 12,000 B.C. Today, bass, trout, gar, paddlefish, catfish, crappie, carp, walleye, muskie, as well as turtles, crayfish, frogs, mussels, and many other forms of aquatic life live in abundance in Ozark lakes and rivers.

And fishing has become one of the major industries in the area, drawing hundreds of thousands of fishermen to these waters annually. The economic effect on this region is immeasurable. This is reflected in the large number of stores and shops that sell bait and fishing supplies, as well as the rod and reel, and lure manufacturers that are around the area. There are also outfitters, guides, and the many marinas that prosper.

But the most obvious development is the national interest that a major sporting goods business in Springfield generated last year, when it held a four-day fishing fair, featuring extensive displays and exhibitions on fishing products and techniques.

The event was so successful that it won't be held this year. The over 200,000 enthusiasts that showed up last year nearly paralyzed the city by congesting traffic and filling up every motel room within thirty miles.

Many of the boats that are manufactured in this area are sold to those same enthusiasts, many of whom fish the area lakes, and enter the numerous fishing tournaments held here.

But the Ozarks provide more resources than just its wild animals. The first Indians used the abundant rocks for making small tools and weapons, to help their hunting and foraging. And during the Woodland period, starting around 1,000 B.C., these Ozarkians began using the clays in the soil to make pottery.

Next, during the Mississippian period, about 900 A.D., they began tilling the soil, and although it's not as fertile as the land to the north, it tied the Indians to this land. The 178 day growing season, along with the forty to fifty inches of rain annually, allowed them to establish homes, no longer completely dependent on following migratory herds and fishing for food.

This same tie with the land continues today, with farming being an important part of the Ozarks' economy. Many present day Ozarkians are involved with the raising of livestock also. Beef cattle, horses, hogs, sheep, and dairy cattle can all be seen in grassy fields along the road. But today, with this snow, they are congregating around feeders and barn lots, waiting out the passing storm.

The grass in the fields is covered with a blanket of cold white snow, so there's no reason for the animals to waste valuable energy looking for it. And the trees stand silent, with their buds dormant, waiting for the warmer days ahead, when once again the warm sun will shine and their leaves will grow, along with an assortment of succulent fruits.

When I was young I worked in a roadside fruit stand. We sold any kind of produce we could get. Although the stands aren't as common as they once were, due to the availability of cheaper produce in the larger grocery stores, they still can be seen along rural roadways, offering freshly picked apples, peaches, pears, grapes, tomatoes, ear corn, potatoes, cabbage, turnips, squash, along with strawberries, blackberries, cherries, gooseberries, blueberries and huckleberries, watermelons, cantaloupes, green beans, etc. Also, smoked hams hang from nails driven into rafters, and Mason jars of honey sit on oak planks.

However, the farmer still has to depend on the regulated agricultural markets to sell his grain products, such as field corn, wheat, sorghum, barley, rye, soybeans, alfalfa seed, lespedeza seed, etc. Mills and grain storage elevators are found in several Ozarks communities.

Another resource for these hills is its lumber. The pine, cedar, and hardwood forests have long supplied inexpensive building materials for the resourceful settlers. Wood, being so abundant, made up almost every part of hearth and home. The tree trunks provided thick, sturdy walls that supported solid rafters, thatched wooden shingles, plank doors, and protected functional, handmade furniture, wooden churns, shelves, tools, bowls, barrels, cooking utensils, boxes, trunks, spinning wheels, even fuel for the fire. Wagons and boats, fences, almost everything needed was made from wood.

And wood is still used to make many products, much of it being sold in the tourism industry in these hills.

As the region has changed, so has the demand for its resources. The iron train rails of the railroads are anchored to wooden ties. As the railroads grew, the increasing need for the wood made the Ozarks a prime lumbering area. A railway spur was built into Chadwick, north of Forsyth, and the timber industry in these hills mushroomed. The boom, however, brought many problems with it.

Chadwick soon saw the opening of brothels, gambling halls, and gin mills that sprung up to syphon off some of the cash flow that was coming into the area. This brought an increase of crime and disorder to the area.

The Baldknobbers formed, and made night rides against these establishments that preyed on the unsophisticated hillmen that were tie hackers. Many of the Baldknobbers made ties themselves.

Lumbering is still practiced in the Ozarks, but not to the degree it once was. Much of the wood that is harvested is now used to heat homes and businesses. Off in the distance I can see a column of smoke rising from a chimney, quickly disappearing into the whiteness of the falling snow.

Another thing that had a great impact on the exploration

and economic development of this area was mining. The Ozarks was, at several different times, covered by sea. The earliest known time was during the Cambrian period, some 550 million years ago. During the 20 million years that this area was an ocean bed, over 1500 feet of rock was formed, laced with lead and copper deposits.

Later, during the Ordavician period, the seas again advanced over this land, this time depositing dolomites.

The third submersion came during the Mississippian period (not the same Mississippian period relative to man's development), when more limestone, the same rock that stands atop Snapp Bald, along with marble, tripoli, lead and zinc were left behind. Later, in the same period, sandstone and shales formed.

The seas covered this region several more times during the Pennsylvanian period, and left more sandstone, shale, and limestone, as well as coal. There were also large deposits of fire clay, making Missouri a leading producer. These clays can withstand temperatures in excess of 3,000 degrees Fahrenheit, making it excellent for containers to store molten metal and glass, as well as lining fireboxes, boilers, furnaces, kilns, and fireplaces.

The French discovered these minerals in northern Missouri in the early 1700's. This inspired Phillipe Renault, a minerologist, to send expeditions into the Ozarks to search for mineral deposits, as well as furs.

Minerals were found in this region, and communities quickly sprung up, basing their whole economies on these mines. A few of these mines and quarries still operate.

Another resource of these hills is the land itself. It was wild and unspoiled, and offered isolation and independence. Since the land wasn't as fertile as lands to the north, the property values reflected it. At first the land price was too inflated, being $1.25 an acre. But the land went unsold, so the Graduation Act of 1854 dropped the price to somewhere between 12.5¢ and 25¢ an acre.

This act provided affordable land to people who wanted

their own homes, which brought another resource to the Ozarks; people.

From the very beginning, Ozarkians have shown a great adaptability to these hills. Out of the virgin timber they built solid homes using simple tools, such as the crosscut saw, axe, adz, froe, drawknife, and cant hook. With wooden dowels, they secured log walls, doors, gates, fences, and furniture with little need of a nail or screw. Walls were chinked with sticks, mud, clay, straw, leaves, or any number of things. Fireplaces were built out of the endless supply of rock that bedeck the landscape.

Pieces of land were cleared, tilled, and planted with numerous staples, each planted at the proper time as was dictated by the "signs." These same crops were also harvested by the "signs."

In order to preserve their harvest, some things were dried, smoked, canned, salted, or stored in a root cellar or cave.

Medicines in these hills were almost nonexistent, so natural medicines found in leaves, roots, barks, and seeds, along with homemade alcohol, moonshine, were widely used.

To provide protein in their diet, they hunted, trapped, fished, and foraged. They also raised hogs, cows, sheep, goats, chickens, and turkeys.

Money, needed only at tax time, since the barter system had long been in use, was raised several ways. People went pearl hunting on the White River, and timbered, trapped, farmed, guided, built, cleaned, cooked, or whatever else was necessary.

For power, natural resources were used. Water wheels were built to turn huge stone grinders, which turned grain into meal and flour. Horses, mules, and oxen were also used to turn the millstones, as well as the sorghum presses that extracted the juice from cane or sorghum. The juice was then boiled down into syrup.

These hill people also devised methods for finding wild

honey. They concocted scented baits that attracted wild honeybees. After the bees filled up on the bait, they would fly directly back to their colony, and the honey hunter would follow. Eventually, after following enough bees, the honey would be found.

To clothe themselves, the hill people tanned hides and furs. They would also spin wool and cotton into yarn, which they would weave into cloth.

Candles, one of the main sources of lighting, were made out of beeswax and beef tallow.

The beds were made from wood, the quilts made from skins and pieced together remnants of cloth, patchwork, and the mattresses were made of straw or feathers.

Clothes were washed by being boiled in iron pots, or scrubbed in a wooden tub, or down at the creek.

Wagons and yokes were also made out of wood.

Everything that could be used from nature was used. Gourds were dried and used to store seeds, painted for decoration, made into bird houses, or into musical instruments, and most commonly, used as water dippers.

They turned clay into pottery. Blacksmiths provided the forged metals that were so important to these settlers. A few of these were guns and shot, knives, tools, wagon wheel rims and hubs, barrel hoops, pots, pans, etc.

Childbirth was aided by the help of midwives or "granny women." I can picture an old woman trudging through the snow on her way to a distant cabin to help a young woman through the perilous time ahead. Though the snow made her steps more difficult, she wouldn't slow her pace, because she was on a mission, one she felt was ordained.

As I walk along slowly through the snow, I think about the spirit that these mountain people had, and that much of that spirit came from their faith, since religion was such an important part of hill life.

These people lived daily with the creation, so they had no reason to doubt the creator. And the church, whether a cabin or brush arbor or cave, offered them spiritual guidance, as well as social interaction, which was needed by these isolated hill folks.

They found ways of turning their everyday activities into social functions as well. They held corn shuckings, house raisings, quilting bees, pea thrashings, hymn singings, log rollings, candy pullings, and hog butcherings. If a large project needed to be done, then these settlers drew from one of their greatest resources, their neighbors.

The resources of this land and its people have proven bountiful, and the bounty continues. These beautiful Ozark mountains that have offered so much to its settlers, are increasingly attractive to people from other areas. The tourism industry is quickly growing into one of the major sources of income. In the Branson area, over four million people visit annually, generating hundreds of millions of dollars in revenue.

But for me the greatest resource in these mountains is the peace I can still find in an oak forest or cedar glade, or following a remote stream to its source, as sparkling waters flow over smooth, flat sandstone rocks. Or the peace I'm feeling as I walk through this fresh, soft snow.

Each frozen crystal flake that falls stacks on top of others, trapping tiny layers of air, making natural insulation for the small animals, plants, and insects that hide below, protecting them from the bitter cold that will follow behind this passing front.

And this snow, when it melts, will provide needed nitrogen and groundwater for the soil and dormant plant life.

I look up into the gray sky and watch as snowflakes materialize, growing ever bigger as they fall in a wobbling, slow spiral toward the ground. I feel their cold wetness as they fall on the exposed areas around my eyes and mouth, quickly melting.

Passing by a high, dark bluff at the edge of the field, I see its differently colored layers that stand as visual evidence of the past changes this land has gone through. Each layer holds secrets of the sea that left it here.

The small outcroppings of rock along the bluff act as shelves, catching small deposits of snow, adding a unique coloration to the rock face.

Beyond the bluff, I can hear the roaring of water as it runs down a ravine below. The only other sound is the soft frozen snowflakes that fall against my coat, and the sound of my feet stepping down on the snow; crunch, pop. Crunch, pop. Crunch, pop.

Behind me, except for my uneven tracks, all other signs of civilization slowly melt away, disappearing in the falling snow, leaving me alone in my peaceful world of white.

Day Five
March 15

In the Rocks

March is a month of diversity. The sign of Pisces shows two fish swimming in different directions. Weather in the Ozarks is well described by that symbol. It can be sunny and warm, and quickly change, becoming rainy and cold. One day calm, the next assailed by gusting winds. And it's not at all uncommon to see early spring flowers with their colorful petals sticking up through a layer of fresh snow.

Today, as I drive into the Mincy Wildlife Area, there is no snow, but I watch the trees swaying in a cold northern wind. I'm not superstitious, but I can remember an earlier time when the 15th of March was ominous. As one soothsayer told Caesar, "Beware the Ides of March." According to the Julian Calendar, this is the Ides.

The forest is starting to get a reddish tint to it as some of the trees are showing their swollen buds as a result of warm days in late February and early March. The grass in the meadows is starting to return to its rich green as life is returning to sleeping stems.

The ground along the river bottom appears to be covered with a patchy green carpet that spreads along the valley floor. Odd assortments of cattle, horses, mules, and sheep graze over the hills, enjoying the succulent beginnings of spring.

I've just come from Murder Rocks, a few miles from here, and I'm looking for a related location. Murder Rocks is an appropriate name for a unique formation of boulders that stand alongside JJ Highway in Taney County. From atop these rocks, the country to the west and north can be viewed fairly easily. When the Carrolton-Forsyth Road passed by these rocks almost 130 years ago, these boulders were an excellent place for outlaws to hide and wait to ambush the freight wagons as they came up the steep northern grade from Forsyth.

Alf Bolin and his men found these rocks to be a perfect vantage point. Alf was, by most accounts, a homicidal maniac. He is credited with killing at least forty people, many of them shot in cold blood. Some of them he saw as an enemy, but others he killed for the pleasure of it.

Bolin, as did many bushwhackers, carried out his reign of terror during the Civil War, when most able bodied men were off fighting. He and his band terrorized this region, committing almost every crime imaginable.

He was in sympathy with the Southern cause, so he committed more crimes against those that were Northern supporters. He would shoot any Union soldier he caught straggling along the road, and would often brag about it.

But he also killed innocent civilians, such as one twelve year old boy he shot while the boy was carrying corn from a field. That was up on Roark Creek. Another time he shot an eighty year old man, "Old Man Bud," who was taking some corn to be ground into meal at the mill for some women in the area whose husbands were gone. Alf forced the elderly man to wade into the creek, where he shot him, leaving his body to float in the water. That was near Forsyth. These same bushwhackers burned many homes in the area, forcing the people to flee.

Alf roamed these hills and it's believed he became quite familiar with the caves and hollows from south of the Arkansas line up to near Ozark, Missouri. There are legends about how he would sneak off to different caves to hide his loot. It is said that he didn't hide it in the caves, but used them as a point of reference from where he would bury the valuables.

These stories seem plausible, because no treasure has reportedly been found, and Bolin obviously couldn't have kept his ill-gotten monies in any bank.

One such cave said to be a hiding place was known as the Fox Cave, in the Fox Hills. I've spent two days trying to find the exact location of this cave. This morning I met with a local spelunker who gave me specific directions, so I'm headng for the site.

Although the wind is still cold, the sunshine is beginning to warm the earth as it shines down on the forest and covers the southern slopes of the hills. Through the trees I can see the early blossoms of toothwort, dog-toothed violets, known by some as trout lillies, dutchmen's breeches, and paw paws.

Birds are gleaning the hillsides, flipping up dried leaves as they hunt for ticks and insects that are hiding underneath. As the soil warms up, more insects will be coming out after a long winter of living underground. Earthworms crawl along the moist ground, offering a valuable bonanza to these feathered treasure hunters.

Passing through an animal feeding site in this protected animal area, I notice the contrasts between the long, dead, brown stems of broom sedge and johnson grass, and the new green growth next to the ground. A few hours ago, before the sun popped up over the eastern hills, this meadow was alive with the fanning of small white tails, as deer fed. The abundance of tracks across the path and near a small catch pond serve as proof.

Having climbed up a very steep hill and then down an equally steep decline, the road turns back up and to the left. At the top of the next hill I find a place to park.

As I step out, I feel a blast of cold wind. The trees twist and bend as gust after gust moves in waves through the forest.

Zipping up my coat and slipping on my gloves, I head off into the woods.

I'm glad that it's cold today, because this is the time of year when snakes begin to burrow out of their hiding places after a long winter of hibernation. As long as the temperature stays low, even if I come across one, it will hopefully be too sluggish to strike.

The three main poisonous snakes around here are the copperhead, *agkistrodon contortrix contortrix*, the western pygmy rattlesnake, *sistrurus miliarius streckeri gloyd*, and the timber rattlesnake, *crotalus horridus linnaeus*, often mistakenly called the diamondback.

The copperhead and pygmy rattler have not been known to kill anyone in Missouri, but the timber rattlesnake is a different story. The state record on one of these is 74.5 inches long. Though the number of timber rattlers has decreased in this area, the last thing I need to do now is run across one, or the copperhead, or pygmy for that matter. These woods are a perfect habitat for all three.

As I move down the southern slope of the hill, the noisy rustlings of my feet through the dried leaves echoes down the hollow. I won't be sneaking up on any unsuspecting animal today.

A few yards into the woods, I reach an odd depression, not unlike a bomb crater or dried up pond, completely covered in leaves. This must be the cave.

I get a long stick and begin prodding around in the leaves, hoping to find the opening without falling in. I can't find it. Maybe the opening, supposed to be nothing more than a crawl way, has collapsed, closing up the cave.

The information I had received was that the cave had been visited in the past six months. We have had some rain and snow this winter which would have caused the cave's ceiling to collapse, but this is probably just a sink hole. I'll just keep looking.

A ravine runs down the hill to my left, so I head off at an angle toward it. Possibly the cave opening is closer to it than I was told.

Walking along, I think about Alf Bolin. He must have been an awfully fierce individual, if the many accounts about him are true. He was said to have been the meanest looking man anyone had seen.

Although my rational mind will not accept the notion of spirits or ghosts, being alone in these woods brings back some of my childhood fears.

If there is a treasure buried in the hills near this place,

does Alf Bolin's ghost guard it? Is he this very moment watching me from some spirit world, his restless soul ever wandering these woods because he was killed before he could reclaim his hidden treasure?

I fight off this paranoia and try to see the humor in allowing such irrational thoughts to creep in. The idea of his ghost is so disquieting that I can't find much to laugh at, so I just push it from my mind.

Making my way slowly down through the trees, I check out every rock ledge that juts out of the hillside. There must be an opening along here somewhere.

I finally reach the ravine and walk parallel with it down the hill. This allows me to look up at both hillsides, but I still can't see the opening to a cave.

I've been searching now for about an hour, and I'm about a quarter of a mile from where I started, which is much further than I should have had to come, so I head back up the hill, again angling to the left. There are so many ledges and boulders, I begin zigzagging back and forth looking for the opening.

Coming up over a rise, not seventy-five yards south of where I found the first depression, I find another bowl-shaped area, only larger, and a bit more conical. I walk along the left edge, until standing on the north rim, I look down and see an opening. It's the cave. I start down into the pit, hoping there is only one opening, and that the dried leaves aren't hiding any traps doors. They aren't.

Reaching the opening, I feel a strange apprehension. So strong, in fact, that I start to shudder. I look around, because it's as though I'm being watched. But I see no one, or nothing, out of the ordinary.

The opening is really nothing more than a narrow fissure that you enter by crawling on your back, until the passage-way opens up into a larger room, large enough to stand up in, with smaller areas off from that. Or at least that is what I was told.

The man had said that the walls and ceiling had been

scratched with names, initials, and other forms of graffiti, left by some that had visited it.

I kick some leaves and uncover a pile of beer cans that must have been left after a party.

Although I'm very curious about going into the cave, my curiousity is now totally negated by the odd sensation of foreboding, so I only poke around the leaves with a stick to see what I might discover.

In a crevice just to the right of the opening, I find a plastic bowl that crumbles as I try to pull it out. Someone must have been using it to dig here. The legend of the treasure is an old one.

If the outlaw did use this cave as a reference point to hide his money, I wonder where it would be. Standing in front of the opening, I look around the woods to see if anything unusual catches my eye, like an unusual pile of rocks or an earth mound.

This thought I do find humorous. I've obviously been watching too many movies, because here I am, standing in the middle of a living, ever changing forest, hoping to instantly find a legendary treasure that would have been hidden some 125 years ago. This is 125 years of falling leaves, trees growing up, and falling down and decaying, along with fire, rain, snow, and erosion, etc.

I guess I expected a shaft of sunlight to come beaming through the trees, setting the hidden cache aglow in supernatural light. Why should it? The sun cares nothing about the money. Or me.

Anyway, at least I've found the cave I've been looking for, the one written about in a story about Alf Bolin, and since he did roam these hills, with Murder Rocks being fairly close, there's a good chance he did visit this cave, because caves have a strange attraction.

What is it about these openings into the earth that draws us? Is it the curiousity of the unknown? Or maybe it's genetic memories of past lives when our ancestors used such places for shelter. Or maybe subsconscious reminiscences of the womb programmed into our developing embryonic brains? The reasons may be unaswerable, but the fact that there is an attraction is apparent.

The Ozark mountains are honeycombed with caves and underground streams. These chambers and waterways provide a unique habitat for certain creatures that long ago adapted to a dark, wet, underground world.

The blind cavefish, *typhlichtys subterranus*, lives in cave streams. Since it lives in total darkness, most of its pigmentation has been lost during evolution, as has its needs for eyes. All that remains of the eyes are two blobs of fat. The fish doesn't need to see because it feeds by using its acute sensitivity to motion.

The cave salamander, *eurycea lucifuga*, is also found in these caverns. But this creature hasn't lost its coloration and its yellowish-orange body with dark brown spots makes it easy to see, should it venture into the light.

Other creatures that live in this subterranean world are the blind crayfish, *orconectus pellucidus australis*, as well as the eastern pepistrelle, dark sided salamander, grotto salamander, pickeral frog, cave cricket, and cave spiders.

These animals live in a very fragile ecosystem that is dependent on the groundwaters that course through the porous limestone of the region.

Whether the cave is effluent, its food chain basis beginning with the nutrients in bat guano, or influent, its food sources being flushed in from the outside world through water runoff, these environments are becoming polluted from industrial wastes, human wastes, as well as farm wastes.

Though this pollution threatens all life forms, it is especially dangerous to the cave dwelling creatures of the Ozarks.

There could very easily be a time in my life when they no longer live out their secretive lives hidden beneath these hills. It will truly be a hidden treasure lost forever.

The bat guano that puts the vital nutrients into the

effluent cave systems in this area comes mostly from the gray bat, *myotis grisescens*, that spends the dark nights combing the air for insects which it catches and eats as it flies.

Gray bat colony sizes average anywhere from 2,000 to 50,000 individuals, with one group reaching 250,000. However, the gray bat population has declined by over 75% in the last fifty years. This is a warning signal of what is to come. Should the bat disappear, so will the cave ecosystems, which will be an incredible tragedy in Missouri, known as the cave state. If the 4,571 known caves in Missouri become lifeless, they will be nothing more than uniquely designed sewers.

Of the 4,500 plus caves statewide, the Ozarks region has a great many, which attracts speleologists and spelunkers alike, the latter being hobbyists. Caving can be very exciting, but also a very dangerous activity, which has cost lives by either accident or error.

Others have found themselves trapped or lost, and had to wait long agonizing hours or days, sometimes in total darkness, to be rescued, with only their pride being hurt.

But the thrill of adventure and breathtaking beauty is, to some, worth the risks. Not me, not today anyway. I didn't leave any message on my vehicle telling where I was going, or what I planned on exploring, which is one of the first rules of caving. Besides, my inner voice is telling me to wait.

It just might be an overly cautious attitude I have today, but long ago I learned to rely on my intuition for many decisions.

I first became acutely aware of it when I went on a pilgrimage, hitchhiking across Canada on summer break from college. The trip had no specific destination and no time perimeters. I just went.

I was astonished at how, when I followed my inner feelings, everything moved along as if on an invisible escalator. Each new ride seemed to arrive on a prearranged schedule, the people being nice, and often going out of their way, unasked, to show me a beautiful view that couldn't be seen from the main road, or to drive through a scenic park. And, almost invariably, at some point during the ride, they would explain with a bit of embarrassed self wonder that they didn't usually pick up hitchhikers. I came to expect the statement.

However, when I went against my feelings, for whatever reasons, the escalator stopped. I could stand at an intersection for hours without much luck, or if I did get a ride, it would turn out to be unpleasant, if not on the edge of being totally dangerous.

After awhile, my feelings became so keen, I would actually turn down rides that didn't feel right. These same feelings, later on during my trip, may very well have saved my life, but that's another story.

Today, the escalator that helped me find the spelunker that knew about this cave is not traveling inside the cave. I can only view the outside. It could be that the warm weather a few weeks ago brought out a poisonous snake that with the cold weather has sought refuge in the cave. Maybe the spirit of Alf Bolin still frequents this place and is not happy with my presence. Or maybe the roof of the cave has been weakened by heavy winter rains, and any disturbance might bring it crashing down. Or maybe I'm just being foolish. Regardless, I'll not find out today.

I sit down on the southeastern rim of the circular basin that's about thirty feet in diameter. The cave opening is just below my feet. Cloud pieces blow overhead as the wind that's carrying them plays in the treetops high on the ridge.

Looking down at the cave's opening, I try to imagine what secrets the rocks below me hide. The countless fissures and seeping springs that carry acidic waters that slowly melt away the rock by picking up calcium and bicarbonate ions, taking them along until the dripping water either evaporates or loses carbon dioixde, leaving mineral deposits behind.

If the deposit is left at the top of a cavity, long hollow soda straw-like formations develop, later thickening and their middles plugging up, until they become stalactites. If the water drops to the floor before losing its mineral cargo then the stalagmites grow upward.

The ever changing calcite formation can resemble coral, building columns, bells, draperies, and they are called such, as well as helicites, or soda straws, or pearls, or any other number of names.

I wonder just how many unique formations are hidden away underground in the thousands of miles of passageways underneath these hills. Some so narrow no one could pass through them, while others are so gigantic large buildings could be erected, or large boats could be floated on their 200-foot deep lakes. The hidden mysteries that lay beneath these hills make me even more thankful to call the Ozarks home.

The sun feels warm against my back as I look up the hill through the trees. So peaceful, so secluded. I wonder if Alf Bolin found this peace. Maybe he sought out these places not to hide his treasure, but to enjoy this solitude; to try and escape the evil forces that controlled him, driving him to commit his horrendous atrocities.

Or maybe this is where he planned his actions, crawling into this cave for shelter, hiding while he planned his next campaign of terror. Only the past knows.

If Alf did hide out in this or other caves, he wouldn't be the first, nor the last, to do so. These caves have offered shelter to animals as well as the Indians, settlers, hunters and trappers, soldiers, travelers, and outlaws of every description.

One such cave carries the name of the bushwhacker who used it. His name was Alfred Cook. He didn't start out as an outlaw, but was just a man who didn't want to get involved with the war. However, he found that he couldn't remain neutral. There were fanatical Union supporters in the area of Taneyville, where he, his wife, and their seven children lived. These Union sympathizers harassed him and his family until they moved across the Arkansas line into Marion County.

Their land was crisscrossed by marauding bands from both sides of the war that took whatever they needed. This put Cook and his family in danger of starvation, so he turned to bushwhacking to survive.

The Union troops scoured the hills trying to find Alfred Cook and his thirteen men. They finally found them hiding in a cave south of Dubuque, Arkansas, which lies between Forsyth, Missouri, and Yellville, Arkansas.

The troops surrounded the cave, ordering the outlaws out, but they refused. The troops then told them they would be treated as prisoners of war, and eleven of them surrendered.

Al Cook, Ed Brown, and Hiram Russell didn't, so the troops built a fire on a ledge above the cave's entrance, and pushed it down into the opening. The smoke from the fire drove the three men out, and they were gunned down and left.

Another bushwhacker that was driven into that activity was Sam Hildebrand. First, his brother was accused of stealing a horse and hanged by the Union militia. Later, while looking for Sam, the militia killed his thirteen year old brother and burned his mother's house.

Sam's bushwhacking became a personal vendetta against the Union. One by one he killed the members of the militia that had "wronged" him and his family. He often took refuge in a cave on a high bluff. Sam Hildebrand successfully eluded capture, and may have lived out his days in these Ozark hills.

Other outlaws that roamed the Ozarks were James and Cole Younger, Frank and Jesse James, Quantrill and his raiders, and John Kelso, a fanatical Union supporter who preyed on any Southern sympathizer. He was later elected to Congress.

John F. Bolin, possibly kin to Alf Bolin, was another

bushwhacker who attacked Unionists. He was captured in 1864 and hanged, but Nathan Bolin and another brother continued the ongoing battle. Their capture was never reported.

The area caves also provided shelter for Al Layton, who shot a Forsyth businessman during a fight. The businessman was a friend of the men who soon after formed the Baldknobbers. Layton was exonerated, one of the reasons the Baldknobbers decided to organize.

But the caves in this area offer more than shelter, they also offer the promise of hidden treasure, just like the one I'm sitting over. The legends concerning these treasures are as varied as the cave formations themselves.

Many stories have to do with Spanish gold, or Spanish silver, lost or stolen from Spaniards who were supposed to have traveled through the Ozarks when Spain owned the region. However, there is very little evidence that they ventured into the Ozarks since it was so inaccessible and inhospitable.

Frank and Jesse James, along with the Youngers, used the Ozarks as a place to hide from the law. So many tales have named different caves as storehouses for their loot. Usually the cave locations are poorly described, or are said to now be under one of the four lakes that are built on the White River, so verification is next to impossible.

But besides being depositories for exotic treasures, caves have served more practical purposes here in the hills. They've been used as shelter from dangerous storms, and have also been used to store fruits and vegetables, since the constant 55-57 degree temperature prevents freezing in the winter, and slows spoilage in the summer.

I wonder again at just what this cave has been used for. Maybe Alf Bolin did use it as a landmark. My eyes close and I imagine the grizzled looking pyschopath moving through the trees, coming to the cave opening. He would look around, to make sure no one was about, and then take his ill-gotten valuables to a secret place where he would bury them, or slide them into an opening under a rock ledge and cover them.

He would probably stay in the area for a while, to make sure no one had seen him, before he slipped back to Murder Rocks, where his gang waited, or he might decide to go to the Foster cabin for something to eat.

The cabin wasn't very far away and Alf frequently went there for meals. Mr. Foster, a Southern sympathizer, had been arrested by Union forces, and was being kept in the Union stockade in Springfield.

The Union soldiers knew that Foster was acquainted with Bolin, so they came up with a capture plan. They told Foster that if his wife would help catch Bolin, they woud set Foster free. He agreed and sent instructions to his wife concerning the plan.

There was a very homesick Union soldier by the name of Zachari E. Thomas, from Iowa, who wanted to go home to his girlfriend. The Army offered him a discharge if he took part in their scheme. He also agreed.

He made his way into the rugged Ozark mountains from Springfield, posing as a Confederate soldier who had escaped from the Union forces. He finally reached the Foster cabin, where he hid up in the loft for several days.

One evening Alf Bolin came by to eat. The young soldier made a noise and Bolin demanded he show himself. The soldier told his story and Bolin apparently believed it, going back to his meal. At some point, the young soldier was able to ambush the outlaw, knocking him unconscious. The two quickly dispatched him.

They sent word of their deed to Forsyth, and the body was recovered. It was to be taken from Forsyth to Ozark for identification, but rather than carry the whole body, the head was cut off, and the body buried somewhere north of Forsyth along the trail.

Whatever secrets he may have had concerning caves and buried treasures died with him. I can only sit here and wonder what may be within arm's reach, or a stone's throw from this place.

The wind is blowing through the trees, but I can't decipher what it is saying. The sun shines down, but there is no bright, glowing beacon disclosing a hidden bonanza.

The water trickles down the ravine behind me, gurgling and falling over the steps of shelf rock that have been washed clean, day and night, year after year, for centuries.

I take a deep breath, feeling the cold, clean air filling my lungs. The world all around me is at peace; serene.

Alf, you may not know it, but I've found your treasure. Not the one you traded lives for, or even your life for, but the real treasure. The one that rides on the wind with the broken pieces of clouds, or washes down the valley toward Fox Creek on the ripples of spring water, or that is starting to grow on the tips of tree limbs, giving off a reddish cast, or that covers these hills and valleys in green and brown carpets, or the intricate world that lies beneath the soil, hidden deep in pockets surrounded by walls of stone. Living. Living.

Yes, Alf, I've found the hidden treasure, and it has been right here in front of me all along.

Day Six
April 20

Shadowy Forces

The buffeting sound of helicopters passing overhead has become commonplace. The past five days of stress are exacting their toll on the people of Taney, Stone, Barry, and Christian counties in Missouri, as well as the folks across the Arkansas state line. Every noise is checked out, every shadow is suspect, as doors and windows are bolted against the unknown.

It is hard to believe that this is the beautiful Ozarks that I've grown to love. It has, for the moment, become an unbelievably bad dream.

It was five days ago that a local state patrolman stopped an out-of-state van for a routine traffic check. Before Jimmy could get to the van, the driver jumped out and opened fire on him with a Mac-10 machine gun pistol, killing him and seriously injuring another trooper. The stranger fled into the dense woods of Taney County, transforming this vacation paradise into a demilitarized zone.

Roadblocks were immediately set up, and an air search began. Then, the news came. The man was believed to be a member of a white supremacist group known as The Order. He was being looked for out west.

Shock swept the area. Why was he here? Were there others here? Was he just traveling through, or was he coming here?

The people in the Ozarks quickly armed themselves. The news media converged on Branson and began trying to unravel the mystery.

The call went out state-wide and hundreds of lawmen, in sundry uniforms, filled the town. Some wore SWAT gear, some combat gear, some hunting camouflage, and others wore their everyday uniforms. They drove all types of uniquely marked city, county, and state police cars.

Motel rooms filled with policemen, the National Guard, and the FBI. Not only was this a search for a cop killer, it was also the beginnings of an assault on an enclave of suspected terrorists, who were hiding behind their religion.

As was later learned, the FBI was already secretly meeting here, planning a move on the white supremacists' camp seventy miles from here, when the trooper was shot. It is believed that the two incidents are not directly related, but as so often happens in these hills, fate added its own strange twist to this story, forcing the lawmen to accelerate their operation.

For several days, my time has mostly been spent around my secured house, within easy access of a loaded 12 guage shotgun, listening to the news and wondering, "Why is that helicopter hovering over the next hollow?" or, "Why is that dog barking?" or, "Was that the wind or someone outside?"

Going about a daily routine in a police state is very difficult. The roadblocks, though in one sense reassuring, in another sense is very intimidating.

The armed policemen weren't playing any games. Even police friends of mine didn't take the time to say much as they approached my vehicle. This was for real. They would walk up, their guns held at the ready, as each possible hiding place was checked.

As I sat in the line of vehicles waiting for my turn to be inspected, I could look into the brush surrounding the hills and see nearly invisible marksmen in full camouflaged gear, ever alert, in case the search of a car might explode into more violence.

I'm sure that many people were unaware of the sharpshooters in the foliage, but I was painfully aware of it.

The manhunt stretched on and on. Terror threatened the community. This man, a neo-Nazi, said to be a trained survivalist, took on an almost supernatural aura as he evaded capture by hundreds of lawmen with the help of helicopters, dogs, special night scopes, search lights, and top-secret spy planes with body heat-sensing equipment.

Part of the fear came because the van that the man was driving turned out to be a rolling arsenal, complete with machine guns, grenades, nitroglycerine, and dynamite. Was this all of his weapons? Or did he have more stashed away somewhere? Was he alone or with others of his group? As the hours dragged on, the unknown terrorized the psyche of the citizens. Paranoia grew.

This scenario was right out of a Hollywood movie, but much worse, because this was real.

This incident is by no means the first terror to be felt in these hills. Of course the natural disasters, such as fire, flood, and diseases, have visited here.

The Trail of Tears passed through here in 1838, when the Cherokee people were forced westward, killing many.

And of course, the terror that the Indians of this region must have felt during the New Madrid earthquake in eastern Missouri in 1811, the worst in United States history.

The Civil War was a horrendous time for the White River area, along with all the human predators that exploited the state of anarchy.

And also, the Baldknobbers on their night rides struck terror in many people.

But here it is April 20, one hundred years later, a time for renewal. The new leaves on these forests of hickory, oak, maple, elm, sycamore, and gum are a bright, beautiful green. The early wildflowers are blooming.

The insects, reptiles, and hibernating animals are coming out after their long sabbaticals. The migratory birds and butterflies that have wintered in the south are making their way back into these mountains.

In the tourist industry, a few hardy vacationers are coming into town despite the obvious state of siege that this community is under.

It's now a month after the vernal equinox, and I'm sitting in my yard enjoying the warm afternoon sunshine.

I become interested in the movements of a honeybee, *hymenoptera*, as it begins to search through the petals of a dandelion. It seems strange that the French would name this small yellow flower "dent de lion," lion toothed.

But though the French named it, it's as Ozarkian as any plant in these hills. Its flowers have been used to make wine, as well as dipped in batter and fried. The leaves are part of the edible green weeds that mountain women have collected every spring to make up what is called "greens." It has always been a welcome addition to diets that lacked sufficient nutrients during the harsh winter months.

If you didn't get your fresh greens, and drink your sassafras tea made from boiled sassafras roots, you just weren't ready to face the heat of summer.

The bee searches through the delicate yellow petals looking for nectar, undisturbed by the yellow pollen that is sticking to the hairs on its legs. It seems like a fair exchange. A payment of nectar for carrying a little yellow pollen to another flower. The bees flies off with its cargo.

Nearby, a double column of tiny red ants move to and from a newly discovered food source. They work as a unit to replenish food supplies that have been depleted through the winter. They show total commitment.

The two columns are nearly straight, only bending to go around a pebble or over a twig. The sunlight glints off the shiny backs of the minute creatures. The two lines seem to pulsate.

A warm breeze gusts momentarily around the yard as radiated heat from the ground causes a momentary inbalance in the air, a swirl of currents until the air settles again. The sun brings a flush to my untanned skin.

Across the hills I can see the blooming redbud trees, interspersed with the white flowering dogwoods. Flying insects reflect the sunlight as they teem over the grass and venture out over the lake.

Robins scurry about, searching for food. They repeatedly rake their claws backwards over the ground, stepping back to examine what their small plowed furrows have unearthed, and then scratching again.

If their hunting isn't successful, they hop, or fly a few feet and try again. They call happily to one another as they scan the ground. But they never drop their state of alert, being ever aware of a possible ambush from a cat or a hawk.

My loaded shotgun is only a few feet away.

A small black beetle hauls its ungamely armored body across the grass, struggling to traverse this obstacle course. It passes right over the double column of ants, each oblivious to the other.

The sound of a helicopter throbs overhead. A Huey transport helicopter. I'm overwhelmed by a sense of deja vu, but I also feel caught up in the surrealism.

This is not a strafing run on an enemy placement in Southeast Asia, not air support for young soldiers pinned down in a firefight, not a troop evacuation from a hostile zone, not a flying interrogation room for a suspected Viet Cong at 1,000 feet above the jungle floor, but still, the helicopter is there, with its guns poised and ready. The flat charcoal green color, moving slowly like a giant flying serpent, ever vigilant, ready to strike.

This is the Ozarks, my home. My base of security. The place I returned to to find peace. The place I need to know and understand.

The helicopter is a dichotomy. Most of the locals see the military presence as a sign of security, and in some ways it is. But few know its desctructive potential.

One Mini gun can fire several thousand rounds of ammunition per minute, striking every quarter inch of earth the distance of a football field. Such overkill.

One fully outfitted gunship could probably do as much damage to this town as all the floods and fires that it has known.

Slowly the helicopter moves on.

I begin to relax again and allow my thoughts to return to the tiny creatures that are moving all about me, not worrying about the potential misuse of power. Here I am, looming high over them, able to destroy their lives with little effort, but they continue on.

The distant sound of the breeze moving through the trees, and the warmth of the April sun, lulls me into a state of lethargy. Spring fever has infected me fully. I close my eyes and let this beautiful setting fill my senses. Birds call in the trees.

At 5:00 p.m. the word comes down. The fugitive has been captured at Shadow Rock Park in Forsyth, not far from where campers were staying. He was either ready to give up, or was waiting for someone. Either way, my relief is obvious, as is the entire area's.

An occasional car horn can be heard as some vent their built up tension behind the wheel of their car, but there is no mass celebration. What is there to celebrate?

There is now a young widow with two small children, whose father, Jimmy, was a friend to this community, killed because he represented, to one man, an agent of an enemy state.

And there is another area lawman recovering from physical wounds, but also wounded in emotional ways that will never fully heal. He will always remember.

And there is the third man, twenty years old, dirty, confused, scared, some say not quite mentally right, covered with ticks and chiggers, scratched, sunburned, hungry, with no future to look forward to. No freedom.

And there is the compound of the group known as the C.S.A., the Covenant, the Sword, and the Arm of the Lord, the white supremacist enclave near here, still at a standoff between lawmen and zealots; both heavily armed.

And there are the hundreds of lawmen who have put in many long, stressful hours manning roadblocks, searching house to house, and combing wooded areas, following up on every lead, from barking dogs to a skinned groundhog, however remote.

Along with the thousands of local people who had their

normal lives disrupted by sleepless nights, continually checking on friends and relatives, and who took food and coffee to officers and troops out in the field.

No, there will be no celebration. Only relief.

My cabin fever finally gets the best of me, so I strike out for a walk along the water. The evening air is still warm. The smell of spring is everywhere.

The air is filled with insects of every description, flying about on their lacey wings, searching out the fulfillment of their preprogrammed instincts: food, survival, reproduction. Carrying and passing along life's baton in a never ending relay race. All in frantic haste.

Relativity. Their lives are limited to hours, days, and weeks, and then they pass that life on, generation to generation.

The currents in Lake Taneycomo move steadily on.

The April sun begins to slip behind the wooded hills. The air is still warm and full of the sweet smell of new foliage, tree pollen, early flowers, and sunshine. The ever present river smell rises from the cold waters.

A fish begins to work the water's edge near the lake bank, slapping a small wave against the shore with a flourish. Other fish can periodically be heard breaking the surface up and down the lake.

Across the water from me is a Great Blue Heron, *ardea herodias*, that's fishing an area of swampy backwater. It slowly steps with its long sharp beak pointed downward as it scans the shallow waters for a movement from a small fish, crayfish, or frog. I watch it as it spears at something, but comes up empty. Water drips from its beak. It fishes for awhile, and I watch it hypnotically until the coming darkness finally persuades it to fly off towards home.

At first, it seems too awkward to fly, as it spreads its huge wings and lunges into the air, dipping dangerously close to the water before gaining altitude, its stick-like legs pumping up and down with each flap of its wings.

But once the heron becomes safely airborne, its legs trail

behind it like rudders and it flies off in smooth, graceful strokes, with only the sound of its wings on the air, and an occasional quacking sound.

The area of backwater that the heron vacated begins to come alive with distinct sounds as the day's final rays of light start to fade.

I've seen nature films that show how frogs inflate their thin throat membranes as they call for a mate. I can't see the frogs or their ballooning throats, but their calls seem to be everywhere.

I can tell the gray tree frogs by their bird-like calls, and I hear the baby chick sounds of spring peepers. The green tree frogs sound more like quacking ducks, but the real croacking comes from the deep voiced bullfrogs. These different pitched singers make for a unique chorus.

All around me the field crickets begin rubbing the front edges of their wings together, making their chirping sounds. The air around me is filling up with the songs of amphibians and insects alike, calling for a mate. The spring cycle is intensifying.

I've always wondered how each specie of frog, insect, bird, and so on, distinguishes one call from another, especially those that sound, to me, very similar. Is it a specific pitch, or tremolo, or a series of sounds that unlocks that instinctive lock? All I know is that something magical happens, or there wouldn't be different kinds of frogs or insects or birds. There might be only one kind of each, or even none at all, since mating would be by a chance meeting, and that might not be enough to work.

Natural selection. Charles Darwin explained what it was in his "Origin of Species," but did he understand just how it was initiated?

I find it amazing that these creatures do communicate through this cacophony of sounds, but I'm even more amazed at how precise the genetic coding must be to carry out the communication. And the different forms of communication used - some use sound, some use scent, some use sight, and odd combinations of all three.

I've read that birds are believed to be directly related to reptiles. I wonder just when, during their evolution, their communication changed from scent messages to sound and sight, or could it be that at one time reptiles called like birds?

The chorus of night creatures stops momentarily as a fish splashes loudly on the water, but the calls quickly start again and regain their intensity.

It's getting dark.

High above, the stars begin to appear in the night sky. This is but one more starry night in the millions and billions of starry nights that have settled over this land.

These stars were seen as signs from the gods, or even as gods themselves to early man. They've been seen as the campfires of dead braves as they journeyed to their idea of heaven.

They've been used as signs for planting, for waging wars, for making every decision concerning living one's life. Superstitions die slowly, if at all. We still read our daily horoscopes, and wish upon a falling star, which of course isn't really a star at all.

These stars that I'm looking up at have been looked at by the Osage, Algonquin, Peoria, Miami, Weas, Piankashaw, Shawnee, Delaware, Cherokee, Missouri, the Spaniard, French, Confederate, Yankee, outlaw, vigilante, and so many others from right here, the Ozark mountains.

And what did they think they were seeing? Did any of them really know? Did they understand that those lights were suns, and that they were very far away? That some of what appear to be stars are actually galaxies containing billions of stars, and that some of those stars are 50,000 times brighter than our own sun star? And that the light itself may have been released into space about the time man was becoming man, and some long before that, the light just now reaching Earth.

As I look up, I wonder how many of those stars are still

there. Or could I be looking at only light that is traveling through space, the star long ago becoming a supernova, and the explosion of light just hasn't reached me yet?

It is so incredible that I can see something that I could never reach, not in one, or ten, or even 30,000 lifetimes, traveling at the speed of light.

And I will never know just how many suns there are in the sky. I know there are over 100 billion stars in the Milky Way, and over 200 billion in the Andromeda Galaxy, and there are tens of thousands of galaxies extending into space for billions of light years. I've heard it said that there are more stars than grains of sand on all the beaches of the world. I can't imagine it!

I also wonder what proto-stars are out there, dust and gas clouds forming into new stars, their density ever increasing until their inner temperatures reach several million degrees of heat, causing a thermonuclear reaction, converting hydrogen into helium, which emits photons into space during the process, turning on another light in the sky.

I wonder what lights have been turned on but their light hasn't reached here yet. I strain my eyes looking into the darkness.

The frogs and crickets call on. They don't worry about the stars, or the moon, or politics. Call a mate. Be on the alert for snakes, turtles, raccoons, cats, foxes, Blue Herons or other frogs, but keep calling. Stake out your territory and call.

I feel a sharp sting on my right arm and I slap at it. A female mosquito has succeeded in providing fresh blood so her next brood will hatch. I wonder which of the over 3,000 species of mosquitoes has just stabbed me.

Down the lake comes the call of the Great Horned Owl, *bubo virginianus*, known locally as the hoot owl. Such a haunting call. It's easy to see why so many people have associated the hoot owl with dark foreboding. I'm sure the sound is foreboding to the small creatures in the night, since the owl is such a formidable hunter. The owl's hearing is so well developed it can hunt in total darkness, homing in on its prey by hearing the heart beating inside the victim's chest.

In the daytime, the slow flying owl is at a disadvantage to the hawk, who competes with it for prey. The hawk will attack the owl during the day, possibly killing it in the territorial dispute. But in the nighttime, the hawk sleeps and the owl is the ruler of the air. Wild turkey, quail, chickens, grouse, mice, and even skunks all become spooked when the Great Horned Owl calls.

I hear it call again, and far off an answer comes back down the valley.

To my right something is rustling through the underbrush. It's probably a fox or a raccoon searching for a meal. I listen as it moves closer, but it stops suddenly. Whatever it is, it has apparently caught my scent, because I hear it turn and move away from me into the night.

My thoughts return to the insanity of the past few days: the killing of the trooper, the siege, the roadblocks, the paranoid people who were shooting at shadows, or the light from someone's cigarette off in a field at night. Or the funeral procession of the murdered officer that was interrupted when a stupid kid, as a joke, ran from his car at a roadblock into the woods, almost causing a catastrophe as armed lawmen, emotionally distraught, stopped their cars and ran toward the thicket, almost running head on into a SWAT team that had been deployed from the other side of the trees. Thankfully, no shots were fired.

And I think about the fugitives, with warrants of all types out for them, that had been hiding out in this area for some time that were caught at the roadblocks. Ironic.

What is it about this land that records historical event after historical event? Are there physical forces involved that attract specific kinds of people to this place, who become famous or infamous? And what part does time play, since many of these occurrences seem to happen at, or nearly at, the same time of year? Maybe the stars have a greater influence than I believe.

April is a prominent month in Ozarks history. On April 10, 1862, there was a Civil War battle at Old Forsyth, which is now Shadow Rock Park. On April 22, 1862, the Union Army set fire to the town. On April 14, 1886, the Baldknobbers of Taney County disbanded, they made the announcement at the same place. This was also where they had earlier broken into the jail, abducted the Taylor boys and took them off to hang.

On April 15, 1927, a great flood devastated the White River Valley, flooding the town. And today, a fugitive from justice, a cop killer, a neo-Nazi, was captured on Hitler's birthday, April 20, at Shadow Rock Park.

Logic tells me that it's only a series of coincidences, but still I have a feeling about it that I can't explain.

There, at Shadow Rock Park, a place the Indians regarded as sacred, where a prehistoric tribe lived in its shadow, where the Osage camped, the Miamis camped, where Mad Buffalo massacred the French and American hunting party, where three Civil War battles were fought, where the Baldknobbers abducted two men who they hanged, where the notorious bushwhacker Alf Bolin had his body taken for identification and was subsequently beheaded, where the town was burned by Federals, where countless floods have washed the land clean, and today it is the place where another historical chapter came to an end. Coincidence?

There is so much in this universe that I don't understand. What sounds the different species of frogs or crickets hear. What draws them together? Or what incredible wonders are only reflected or hinted at in the night sky. What strange happenings occur time after time in this land called the Ozarks, some for a reason, some unexplained, but still changing history forever just the same.

One thing I do know, it's getting late. I'm growing tired of supplying mosquito mothers with my life's blood, and the night is growing chilly.

Tonight I can finally relax and sleep a solid sleep. I'll let the strange sounds go unchecked as my mind surrenders to dreams.

No more questions or wonderings. No more 3.8 million foot-candle helicopter searchlights flashing across the hills and valleys, invading the serenity of the darkness.

For now, the Ozarks night has been returned to the stars.

Day Seven
May 20

To Rise From the Earth

A warm breeze blows through the treetops as the lush green leaves sway in the morning sunshine. The sweet smell of newly mown grass attracts hordes of insects of every description that crawl, jump, or fly from stem to leaf to stem, looking for food or a mate.

The 80 degree mark will easily be reached today as the Ozarks is under the influence of a strong high pressure system. It might even get up to 88 degrees. The weather forecast is calling for rain by the end of the week, but for now there is just lots of sunshine, as plants are exploding up out of the ground, fueled by the carbohydrates created by the magic of photosynthesis. The sun is really making the chlorophyll work overtime.

The oxygen that all of these green plants are giving off seems to work as a stimulant. I feel a need to do something active, so I'm going to spend the day hiking some trails near Table Rock Lake.

The trails weave in and out through forests of oaks, elms, locusts, cedars, sassafras, buckthorns, hickories, wild grape vines, chinquapins, and walnut trees. The undergrowth is made up of saplings, shrubs, dead logs and leaves, lichens, mosses, wild grasses and flowers, and the ever present poison ivy that flourishes in these hills in the summertime.

Water from wet-weather springs seeps through the decaying leaf matter, feeding various forms of bacteria and fungi, which hastens the breakdown of the leaves, returning the borrowed elements to the earth for re-use.

Snails, worms, frogs, spiders, snakes, skinks, and many other creatures thrive in the ecosystems of the forest's floor. Insects are everywhere.

Entering the woods, I'm met immediately by several

gnats that have picked up my scent, and swarm around my face and head, darting in and out, looking for a chance to get a taste of whatever it is they smell, probably the butyric acid in my sweat that is standing in beads on my forehead, and on the nape of my neck.

These pests often intrude on my visits to the woods, hovering around my face, investigating my ears, eyes, nose and mouth. Too often, these "kamakasi" insects fly too close, and crash into an open eye or ear.

Sure enough, as I start my walk, one finally commits "jisatsu," slamming into my left eye, which starts to burn as it jerks shut. I hold my hand tightly against the eyelid, keeping it from blinking involuntarily, which would only spread whatever chemical it is that the dying gnat is secreting, making it burn more.

I wait for my lachrymal gland to produce enough tears to wash it out, fighting off a wave of anger as the burning in my eyes and the partial blindness leaves me feeling helpless and extremely frustrated. A tiny terrorist has struck again.

All I can do is hold my eye and wait, and make sure I don't lose my other eye to another fanatical flyer. After a few minutes that seem more like hours, the intruder's body is washed out, and my watering, bloodshot, out of focus eye can be used again.

I move on slowly, waiting for my vision to clear, and decide that the inconvenience of the gnat is really a small price to pay for enjoying the woods that are so beautiful this time of year. I don't want to pay too often though.

The path is dappled with the sunlight that leaks through the leaf canopy overhead. Flitting in and out of the leaves are birds totally involved in mating and the building of nests. A robin stops on a limb long enough to call, and then flies off through the undergrowth, totally unconcerned about my presence. The calls are all around.

Off to my left there is a rustling in the dried leaves. I stop, thinking I might see a squirrel or chipmunk looking for seeds. As I locate the movement, I can see that the leaves aren't being tossed about, as squirrels and chipmunks do, but instead are slowly being bulldozed from underneath.

The culprit is quickly discovered as a small orange, snake-like head periscopes up through the leaves. *Terrapene carolina triunguis*, the three-toed box turtle, is either searching for insects, mushrooms, earthworms, new leaves, or looking for a female. The bright orange head and neck distinguishes this one as a male.

I remember catching these reptiles as a kid, using them as living toys. We would have races, or paint the scutes of their shells different colors and enter them in pet contests. This one I'll leave alone, although I'm a little curious to know if its back feet do indeed have three toes, or four as some others do. Maybe another time I'll look.

These animals are quite adaptable, ranging over much of the state, and although many die on the highways or during the winter if they can't dig deep enough into the soil, nature has given them extra tools for survival. One is that a female can carry sperm inside of her up to four years, able to produce fertilized eggs that will hatch, thus allowing them to control reproduction. This is extremely beneficial, should a period of scarce food supplies make survival of the offspring extremely difficult, or if there should develop a scarcity of breeding males.

The olive brown shell with the yellow lines radiating from the center of each scute makes these little tanks not only attractive, but very well camouflaged in the ground cover. It slowly plows on, sliding along on its slick, hinged, plastron bottom.

As I watch the turtle move slowly away, I notice a small brown, translucent casing on a nearby tree trunk. Then I see another and another. Not just a few, but hundreds of empty casings. They are attached to the undersides of leaves or to limbs, tree trunks, or anything else that would work. I've seen cicada husks before, but not in such large numbers.

These husks are the dried outer skins of cicada nymphs. Once the insects burrow out of their ground nurseries, they attach to a limb or a leaf, or whatever. Their outer skin splits along the back, allowing the cicada to crawl out of the old skin. The husk remains attached to the support as the insects transforms itself by unfolding its new wings, stretching them out. It pumps blood into these venated membranes, and waits as the night air dries and hardens them.

Once these wings have dried, the cicada leaves its old skin behind, moving to the tops of nearby trees, where, along with thousands of other cicadas, a frantic mating cycle begins.

After the fertilization, the females use their needle-like ovipositer to inject their eggs into twigs and branches. This is about the only damage the cicadas do to their tree hosts, and this damage is minimal.

Once the eggs hatch, the tiny ant-like nymphs fall off to the ground, burrowing into the soil and attach themselves to the roots which they feed on. They stay affixed to these roots most of their lives, until some unknown force signals them to return to the surface.

There are some 1,500 species of cicada, but only three types live in the Ozarks - the annuals, the thirteen-year, and the seventeen-year. The annuals don't come out until June, and the last seventeen year cycle was just a few years ago, so these must be the thirteen- year variety.

Looking down at the ground, I see hundreds of perfectly round holes everywhere. I'm really sorry I wasn't here last night. What an incredible happening. I can just imagine hundreds and thousands of bulging- eyed insects burrowing out of the ground in the dark hours of the night, climbing up vegetation, and molting their skins. All of this happening at the same time, all according to a hidden genetic clock that was programmed in each nymph thirteen years ago, or maybe even programmed millions of years ago in the first thirteen-year cicadas; the DNA passing the message on, generation to generation, that it was to happen last night. And it did.

All that remains of this miracle, besides the ground riddled with finger-sized holes, and the brown, dried husks of the "magicada," are the amorous adults, swarming in the treetops, living out their brief adult lives in orgiastic fervor.

I continue to look under the lower leaves of nearby bushes to see how many casings are attached to each. Very few leaves have not been used. These casings will remain until the wind or rain eventually knocks them loose. Already some have fallen, returning to the earth again. I move on.

Occasionally I run into an invisible spider web that was draped across the path during the night. Each time one sticks to my face or arms, I stop and pull it off. Since I can't see them, I reach where I think they are, and my exaggerated motions resemble that of a street mime, picking up an imaginary object.

Deeper into the woods, the webs become more common, until I finally pick up a stick and wave it up and down in front of me to clear the way as I walk. This entire drama, the pulling off of invisible webs and the waving of my stick wand, undoubtedly looks like the exortations of a mountain shaman warding off evil spirits, or just the actions of a madman. I'm glad no one is around to see.

My movements haven't gone totally unnoticed, however. From somewhere in the trees comes the threatening cry of a bluejay, *cyanocitta cristata*. From its agitated calls I decide I must be close to where it is nesting and it's letting me know I'm violating its territory. Several others join in the challenge, and they move from limb to limb, coming as close as they dare, trying to drive me away. It seems a little early in the summer for such reactions, but I quickly move on to diffuse the situation.

The sound of my steps on the gravel path are quickly absorbed by the surrounding vegetation. I listen closely, and my feet sound farther away than they really are. It's almost like floating.

The trees along the path are still displaying discarded cicada husks here and there. One tree, a post oak, not only holds its share of casings, but it also displays a strange set of scars that run up its entire trunk. From the way the bark has been torn away in wide strips, it's apparent that the tree has been struck by a bolt of lightning.

The millions of volts of electricity that passed through this natural lightning rod superheated the water in it, which turned to pressurized steam, which literally blew the strips of bark away. Insects have already begun to work on the exposed areas. Every opportunity in nature is exploited.

The path skirts the right bank of a small catch pond, still mostly full from the spring rains. The bottom of the pool is covered with dead leaves, partially buried in silt. Tiny black tadpoles swim around the warm water. In one end of the pool a film of pollen has collected on the surface. The wind has pushed it against the bank, and it resembles loose, yellow, wrinkled skin, bunched up on the water.

This small pool will be a prime breeding ground for mosquitoes. Fresh tracks show that it is also a stopover for deer during the night. There are other tracks that indicate a raccoon has checked the edges of the pond for food.

Not far beyond the pond the trail opens into a small meadow. May is a beautiful time for the profusion of wildflowers that adorn these hills.

Spring beauties, anemones, may apples, shadbush, wild plum, black cherry, bladdernut, wild strawberries, wild hydrangea, queen anne's lace, to name a few, bloom widely, supplying bees, butterflies, moths, and hummingbirds with plenty of nectar. In Missouri there are 1,882 flowering plants, not counting the grasses, sedges, and weeds whose blooms are not noticeable without closer examination.

Nearing the glade, I pick up the sweet smell of azalea,

rhododendron roseum, sometimes called honeysuckle. The pink groups of trumpet-shaped flowers are very popular with insects.

Finding a comfortable spot, I sit in the warm sunshine and watch the activity around the plants. Bees, of course, are busily going about their work. However, I'm also treated with the appearance of a spicebush swallowtail butterfly. Its black wings greatly accentuate the white, yellow and bright blue markings. It slowly fans its wings up and down as it feeds from the blossom.

When we were kids, we'd catch butterflies and lightning bugs, putting them in jars so we could watch them more closely. Too often, though, the butterflies were injured during capture and their damaged wings left a powder the same color as the wings on our hands. I remember how, looking at my colored hands, I would feel ashamed of hurting something so unnecessarily. My observations are now done from a distance.

This time of year the Ozarks are full of many kinds of butterflies and moths, along with their strange looking caterpillars.

Many species of swallowtails are shaped a great deal alike, and except for their unique colorations are obviously related. However, their caterpillars are different in almost every way. In this area, there are the spicebush swallowtail, tiger swallowtail, as well as palamedes, giant, Missouri woodland, parsnip or black, zebra, tailless, and the pipevine or blue. Looking at the extreme similarities of the adults, it makes the miracle of metamorphosis an even greater wonder.

The butterfly flies up off the azalea, hovers for a moment, and then slowly flies off.

I think about getting up myself, but a sudden movement stops me. At first it appears to be a bumblebee or a moth, but as soon as it stops in mid-air, I can see it's a hummingbird. It appears as if it is suspended in air as its body, except for the blur of wings, is completely motionless.

It's a ruby-throated hummingbird, *archilochus colubris*, that is scanning the azalea's blossoms to see what treasures they hold. I'm not sure if it is looking or smelling, but it ascends a little, moving in for a closer check.

These tiny birds are common in the Ozarks. It's not unusual to see bright red hummingbird feeders hanging from porches and tree limbs around houses. A lot of people sip their morning coffee while watching these minute birds feeding on sugar water dispensed from tubes disguised as large flowers.

The beautiful colors of the hummingbird shimmer as its feathers refract the sun's rays, breaking them down into their color components. A rainbow on the wing.

It is believed these birds started out in South America, beginning as insect eaters some three million years ago, but have evolved to live mostly off nectar today.

Baby hummers are still fed insects. Right after birth, their mother begins catching about 100 insects on an outing, and brings them back to the fledgling. She makes about twenty outings a day, so the baby receives approximately 2,000 protein-rich insects every day.

Their diet is changed to nectar during the last few days in the nest to increase necessary energy levels to allow the babies to fly out.

This childraising is extremely difficult for the female who has been left to build the nest and raise the brood right after mating. She usually has 2 pea-sized eggs in each clutch. Since hummingbirds require vast quantities of food to sustain life, the female must reduce her body temperature during incubation, which reduces her need for food.

Much of the bird's energy needs are due to its incredible heart rate, which beats 1,200 times per minute while flying, and 480 times per minute while at rest. This high energy output requires the tiny creature, which weighs less than a nickel, to replace its food supplies every ten to fifteen minutes throughout the day.

This need for continual feeding would make nighttime a disasterous situation were it not for the bird's ability to go into a state of night hibernation, or torpor, which slows the heart rate down to 36 beats per minute, and drops the body temperature from 110 to 55 degrees.

How these eating machines make it to Patagonia, near Tierra Del Fuego, every winter, and return every spring, is a total mystery, but they do.

As I watch, the tiny bird flits around the blossoms, and either not finding what it's looking for, or not comfortable with my presence, it quickly disappears.

The gnats have found me again, so I decide to move on myself.

Stepping into the shade feels cool as the breeze begins to evaporate my perspiration. The dappled sunlight on the forest's floor makes a perfect hiding place as a five-banded skink, a kind of lizard, scurries across the path and disappears into the undergrowth.

A rock beside the trail is covered with patches of moss and lichens. These lichens that can live almost anywhere are quite unique plants. Part algae and part fungi, they can live on rocks, trees, dead plant matter, or just about anything. The fungus part of the plant uses an acid to dissolve the rock or wood, or whatever, to supply the needed nutrients for the alga. The alga, in return, supplies CO_2 for the fungus to survive. The best of both worlds in one plant.

A group of black-eyed susans are growing near the rock. They, too, are being courted by summer suitors: bees and butterflies. A small white butterfly walks over the petals of one of the flowers. I'm not exactly sure just what kind it is, but I think it's a female spring azure in her summer coloration. Since there are over 100,000 species of butterflies and moths, I study the small insect for a few moments, trying to memorize distinguishing characteristics to help with later identification.

I may even find a picture of it in its larval stage. Caterpillars of many descriptions are hatching out of their eggs and are searching the forests for food. Most of the larva eat leaves, but some feed on stems or trees. Some also eat flowers or fruit or lichens, dried leaves, or decayed wood. A few kinds live on animal fur, feathers, and wool clothing. And one kind lives on bat guano. The decreasing bat population will affect yet another life form.

There is only one carnivorous butterfly larva in the United States and that is the harvester butterfly, which feeds on wooly aphids.

When the caterpillars aren't eating, they make a tent from a leaf, hiding inside. They also make these tents during bad weather. The caterpillars, which are also tiny eating machines, finally molt their skins for the last time and become dormant, which is now the pupal stage. The butterfly pupa forms a chrysalis, but the moth pupa either spins a cocoon or pupates in an underground chamber.

Here in Missouri, butterflies hibernate as pupae, and emerge in the spring as fully developed butterflies, or imago.

Some butterflies, such as the monarch, migrate to the south every fall and return with the warm sunshine. Millions of orange and black wings can be seen slowly making their way through the Ozarks twice a year. Since the monarch is somewhat distasteful to eat, birds quickly learn that these brightly colored insects aren't worth the side effects, and what would otherwise be a veritable feast for the birds turns out to be an aesthetic feast for the observer.

The small butterfly works on, not caring if I watch or not. I move on.

The trail comes to another clearing at the lake's edge. The rocky ground slopes down to the water. I leave the path and follow the slope to where the small windblown waves of water splash against shelf rock.

Looking out across the water a few hundred yards, I see

a small island covered with the trees that were growing there when the lake waters rose, isolating them from their relatives on both sides of the lake.

It reminds me of island chains, such as the Galapagos Islands, where the animals and plants were isolated by rising seas and how they evolved into unique creations, much different from their distant relatives.

This island is not isolated enough to evolve different plants and animals, but the idea is an intriguing one. If the air and water between here and there were impenetrable by seeds, pollen, birds, or animals, it would be interesting to see what effect a few million years of inbreeding would have on that same hilltop island; what unique ecosystems would evolve, and what combinations of adaptability would come into play.

High out over the lake a lone mallard is flying. It glides for a ways and then starts its descent towards the water. A few yards above the surface it begins flapping its wings as it leans backwards, slowing its forward motion. It stretches out its webbed feet to make contact with the water. Once they touch, it glides on them for a moment and then splashes down as its body makes contact. Although it's alone, it will probably be joined by others before too long.

I bend over and pick up a flat piece of chert. I spin the rock out over the water, watching it skip across the surface.

I've spent long hours walking along lake shores, or stream banks, looking for smooth, flat rocks that skip the best. It is very relaxing to skim stones.

I try throwing a few more, but the wind is blowing the waves in toward me, and they rise up and grab the skimming rocks prematurely. I'll wait for a calmer day.

For a moment, I recall another May day one hundred years ago. I wonder what the weather was like then, when the Baldknobber era finally ended with the hanging of the three Baldknobbers at Ozark. I'm sure it wasn't anything like today. With the terrible spectacle taking place, I'm sure no one was listening to the wind blowing through the trees, or the birds loudly calling for a mate. And the warm sunshine undoubtedly turned hot and uncomfortable to the thousands that crowded together to watch the terrible ordeal, the botched hanging which finally took 35 minutes to end the three lives.

I look out again toward the mallard, but it is still alone; a small dark spot floating on the water.

Following the lake shore to the south, I round a bend and come to a small cove. The cove is dotted with tree stumps that stick out of the water. They are all that remains of the forest that unluckily lay in the path of the newly formed lake's waters. Around the cove is a thicket of brush, weeds and briars.

Near the edge of the water, where the weeds are the thickest, I see a movement. As the weeds part, a small muskrat appears as it heads toward the water, hitting it with a splash, and diving out of sight.

I stand still and wait. A few moments later, a small brown head with black eyes resurfaces a few yards away. It watches me intently.

The White River was a perfect home for muskrats, but I've not seen any living on this lake, although I'm sure they still live along the lake's tributaries.

The muskrat, *ondatra zibethica*, is really misnamed, since it's not a rat at all, but is a relative of the field mouse. Muskrats, though not very big, produce a thick brown fur. They usually build their houses out of plants or burrow into stream banks below the water, with the living chambers opening up underground, above the water line. Flooding is one of the biggest threats to these rodents, along with predators like the mink, hawk, and snapping turtle.

Muskrats are very prolific animals, mass reproduction being the rule, which causes eat outs, meaning there is too large a population for the local food supplies.

When this over population does occur, usually in the fall, the muskrats, which are less vulnerable in the water, are often forced to strike out overland, up to twenty miles, looking for a pond or stream with adequate food supplies.

This muskrat must be looking for a new home. I'm not sure, since I can't see any signs of a structure and the lake bank is too rocky to burrow into.

Sometimes the muskrat babies are abandoned by their mothers or are preyed upon by their fathers, but because so many offspring are produced, the small mammals flourish.

This fur bearer, though not as highly valued as the beaver, is still harvested for its pelt. Approximately ten million skins are taken annually, adding $35 million to the economy. Also, the meat is sold commercially under euphamistic labels such as "Marsh Hare," or "Chesapeake Terrapin." The fur is often marketed under the misnomers "Red River Seal," "Hudson Seal," or "River Mink."

The muskrat, its head barely above the water, apparently doesn't appreciate my interested stare, so it dives again, swimming away underwater to some secret, more private place.

The noonday sun is really starting to bear down. My skin is already starting to flush, so I retreat back into the woods and shade. Finding the trail again, I continue on. Since these paths wind around, I will eventually return to the starting point.

I'm walking again, but at a faster pace, apparently becoming somewhat bored with my outing. It's strange that my senses are so quickly dulled to things around me, things that an hour or two earlier would have demanded my full attention. But now, I walk past them, giving only a brief look, my mind thinking thoughts of personal things far away.

The analytical side of me tries to understand why my appreciation for these beautiful Ozark mountains can at times be so ephemeral. On one day, I'll sit for hours atop a tower or rock ledge looking out over a gorgeous valley, filling myself to the soul with a sense of elation and awe; in unity with the world and its creator. But the next day, I may pass by this same valley, my mind focused on some banality, and this beautiful place goes totally ignored. Only a backdrop, a stage setting for a meaningless, second rate drama to be performed; a mundane story, with mundane actors, in a heavenly setting.

It's strange how that familiarity, in this context, doesn't necessarily breed contempt, but rather apathy. I too often take these hills for granted.

The trail continues to wind through the trees, coming near a roadway. I again leave the trail and work my way carefully through some briars to a clearing where I quickly climb up the road embankment.

From the road, I can see the hills to the east and Lake Taneycomo winding its way toward Forsyth. The hills are dotted with homes and buildings as this area continues to grow.

On a distant hill, one structure stands out. It's the Hyer Bell Tower and Williams Memorial Chapel at The School of the Ozarks, just down the valley a few miles. This bell tower and adjoining chapel remind me of the Gothic-styled churches found in Europe. The tall limestone bell tower stands above the trees that overlook Lake Taneycomo far below.

The School of the Ozarks is a four-year college that has evolved quite a bit since its inception in 1907. It has undergone many changes and has overcome many hardships, as it continues to do, but it still remains a symbol of the sturdy Ozarkian spirit that it was built on.

James Fulton Forsythe, not related to the Forsyth that gave his name to the Taney County seat, made his way to Forsyth in June of 1901. He was a Presbyterian missionary. After he arrived, he saw the need and desire for education, so he began teaching school. He formulated a plan for a regional boarding school for the impoverished hill people.

The planning and financing of this facility took several years, but his dream was realized when the school was opened in 1907 in Forsyth. The school taught the common grades as well as high school, boarding both male and female students from throughout the Ozarks region.

In January of 1915, the main school building, Mitchell Hall, was destroyed by fire. The school reopened six days later, using makeshift facilities to finish out the school year.

Another site was located which offered more land and opportunity for growth. So in September, 1915, the school was relocated to its present site, using what was known as the Old Main Clubhouse, already there, as its main building. This became known as Dobyn's Hall. Additional buildings were added in 1917.

Dobyn's Hall burned in February, 1930, but the school continued to go and grow. The chapel and bell tower were built around 1958. But another fire struck in December, 1964, taking the A.P. Green Building.

Despite its setbacks, the school is still going strong, though now it is strictly a college, where students work their way through. This school has a rich heritage, and was instrumental in bringing education to a poor, isolated region of America.

The school is now having to reorganize in order to deal with financial problems, but I have a feeling it will weather this crisis also. Because the resilience this school has shown over the years is the same resilience that is dominant in the land and the people of the White River region; sometimes having setbacks, but never giving up.

I let my eyes follow the horizon back toward the north and west. Off to my left, another butterfly maneuvers through the air, searching for another blossom. These insects are such delicate creatures, yet so intricate and complex.

Their Greek name is Lepidoptera, which means scale

wing. As I watch the butterfly ride the wind, I again think about the migrating monarchs. Hundreds of thousands, moving south, flying along at an unsteady pace, looking so fragile and helpless.

It's so hard for me to imagine them flying for thousands of miles, some coming down the west coast, some coming from New England and eastern Canada, and even more coming down through the central United States, all arriving in the mountain forests of Mexico, within a thirty to fifty mile area, somewhere south of the Tropic of Cancer.

These migrants huddle together in huge masses, trying to survive the mountains' weather. When the winter is extremely harsh, or the forests have been carelessly cleared, eliminating protective cover, many of them die, usually those on the outer edges of the mass of bodies.

But as the sun moves back toward the north in the spring, the surviving monarchs return to their summer homes.

Somehow, preprogrammed in intricate detail, these journeys are predestined. Aside from having to survive in a very unpredictable world, each step's instruction is locked away in a secret place, possibly the DNA, using a secret code.

These butterflies begin as eggs, hatching into caterpillars, who, after molting, become pupae, and eventually emerge as butterflies. But this is not enough. They must also run the gauntlet, traveling to distant, unseen places because it is their destiny; acting totally on instinct.

How am I so different? I shouldn't be. However, I have been given a brain that can work somewhat independently of my preprogramming. It's an over-ride system which I may too often use. I too often envision myself as omnipotent or omniscient, which makes me even more vulnerable in this unpredictable world. A world where the passing of natural law is final.

I feel a strong need to get back in touch with my programming. To follow my heart, and not so much my mind. I need to be content like the caterpillar, to crawl and feed and wait. And when it's time, to form my chrysalis and then emerge with my wings.

But flight is not enough. I must also make the sacrifice of struggle, purely on faith, to that place where my heart bids me to go.

The kind of faith that raises trees from seeds, that sends the muskrat searching for a new home, that built The School of the Ozarks up from the earth, that brings the cicada out of its earthy tomb to fly above the trees, and the faith that sends the monarch on its epic journey.

I still have a long way to go.

Day Eight
June 23

An Inspiring Land

The beam of light from my flashlight pierces the darkness of the night.

It's early morning and I'm making my way up the winding pathway towards the top of Dewey Bald Mountain and to the observation tower there.

The light illuminates the narrow walkway and the trees that line both sides, casting strange, moving shadows that circle around me as I pass by.

Occasionally I shine the light to one side or the other, to make sure the dark movements are only shadows, but usually I try to keep my light straight ahead to make sure I don't step off the path or step on a snake that might be taking advantage of the warm asphalt.

As I get nearer to the top of the hill, the path forks and I take the trail to the right, which is nearer to the tower.

The stars are quite bright tonight, and seem to be playing peek-a-boo with me through the heavily leafed trees.

A moth has found the light, and circles around it, and my hand. Now and then it brushes my skin.

The trail continues upward in a large sweeping circle around the right side of the mountain. The distance isn't far, but the steep angle of ascent makes it a slow climb, and it seems farther than it actually is. My breathing is getting a little heavier.

As I near the upper part of the hilltop, the trees on the right side of the trail disappear, allowing the bright stars in the night sky to fill my view. They seem even brighter as the darkness of Mutton Hollow below adds contrast to their white light.

The path turns back to the east and I do a quick forced march on to the top, where directly in front of me the gray metal tower reflects the light from my flashlight.

The crickets are calling to each other around the hillside, unconcerned about me or my flashlight. Off down in Mutton Hollow the night call of the whippoorwill echoes through the trees. I don't think nature has a more beautiful singer. I listen for a while, as the stars shine and twinkle in the sky.

I start up the six flights of the tower. Each time I've reached the top of one flight, and turn around to go up the next, my view of the sky is expanded. The trees that surround the tower keep getting lower and lower, as the stars spread farther in all directions.

The top of the tower is an open observation deck, surrounded by a four foot wire mesh retaining fence. I finally reach the top and I'm immediately met by the open, domed, star filled sky that encircles me, making me feel as if I'm floating away. It is breathtaking. I slowly walk around the deck, taking in the incredible view of the heavens, as the crickets chirp below and the whippoorwill calls again.

Off to the southeast, down below my observation point, the bright street lights along Highway 76 and the town of Branson shine on, attracting huge swarms of insects that spend whole nights (which for some are their whole lives) circling and diving, climbing and circling again, trying to reach the unattainable source of light. The light they don't understand, but that they apparently need, to the degree that they will die in the struggle to reach it. From here the tens of thousands of tiny wings reflect the light and look like small, pulsating clouds; expanding, contracting, expanding, contracting.

Every once in a while a car drives along the highway below, and I watch it as its taillights go out of sight around a curve, and I listen as the sound of its engine and its tires against the pavement slowly fades away.

This early in the morning, the driver is probably a breakfast cook in one of the many restaurants who wants to get an early start before the tourists wake up and start their day.

Branson, which now has around 5,000 permanent residents living in and around the outskirts, is visited by over four million tourists every year, the vast majority coming betwen April and November. They fill many of the over 9,000 motel rooms that are available. Staying one or two days or a week, and some even staying longer, they clog Highway 76 between Branson, 5 miles to the east from where I'm standing, and Silver Dollar City, about three miles to my west. This traffic is often bumper to bumper from nine o'clock in the morning until, sometimes, past midnight. Seeing the highway empty right now seems so unnatural, but nice. Right now there is no smell of exhaust fumes or screeching tires, or roaring engines and honking horns, only the sweet smell of summer, and the crickets and whippoorwills.

The fleeting shadow of a night creature passes by in the sky, but is quickly gone.

Off to the southeast, beyond the streetlights of the highway, are the approach lights to the airport at The School of the Ozarks. From my tower, I look directly down the runway. I have the same view as an incoming pilot on final approach, who looks down at the two lines of blue parallel perimeter lights.

My view drops from the runway back down to the highway, where flashing neon lights advertise motels, restaurants, music shows, gift shops, go-cart tracks, and water amusement parks.

It would seem that all of the Ozarks is located on this narrow strip of asphalt that runs about ten miles through these hills, since most of the people who come here to vacation spend much of their time sitting in the slow moving traffic or standing in line for food and entertainment. It's a shame that most of them won't really get to know the Ozarks.

Another car appears on the still sleeping road, coming from Branson toward my mountain, passing by just below. I turn and watch it as it skirts the hillside, traveling along the ridge above Mutton Hollow, finally going over the crest of a hill near the Shepherd of the Hills Homestead.

The Shepherd of the Hills Homestead, and the outdoor drama that is performed there nightly, is based on the book, "The Shepherd of the Hills," written by Harold Bell Wright. It is one of the major reasons tourism is so strong here.

The book was written in 1907, based partly on old Ozarks' stories that Wright had been told by local hill people, but it also had strong similarities to parts of Wright's own life, which was one of extreme adversity.

Harold Bell Wright was born in May, 1872, in Rome, New York. His father, William Wright, a Civil War veteran, had returned home after the war as a hero, but couldn't adjust back to civilian life. He became an alcoholic, unable to hold down a job. The family was very poor.

Harold's mother, Alma, died when he was only eleven years old. After staying with different relatives, some of them kind, others not so kind, he returned to his father. This stay was short lived, and at the age of twelve, he had to start working to support himself. Things started looking better for him, but his father got involved and it all fell apart.

Harold was so overworked and malnourished as a child that he was very susceptible to illness and suffered from pneumonia, malaria, and tuberculosis, along with other respiratory problems. He was near death several times.

His father would sometimes find work, and when he did, he would send for Harold. They finally wound up in Findley, Ohio, an oil boom town, living with four of his father's army buddies above a saloon. Harold had to cook and clean for all of them. From his accounts, the lifestyle in that town was anything but civilized. One day he found a man lying at the bottom of the stairs with his throat cut, and no one seemed to notice.

His only friend was a deformed dwarf woman who cooked in a house of prostitution next door. They would talk to each other through their adjoining windows.

Finally, Harold couldn't tolerate his father anymore and hopped a train, getting off in another part of the state. That was where his life began to change.

He had never been exposed to religion, but one day he went to listen to a visiting evangelist preach, and became "fired" [3] by the message. Harold became involved in a church, although he didn't necessarily ascribe to the beliefs of a certain denomination.

An unknown benefactor offered to pay for his education, and he started attending Hiram College in Hiram, Ohio. It was a denominational school of the Disciples Church, and although it was called a college, it was really "something less than high school." [4]

Harold quickly became disillusioned with the human frailty of the supposed elite of the academic and religious community, but he didn't let that interfere with his faith. However, after his second year of school, he became ill and his doctor suggested he not return to the school.

He decided to visit some of his relatives who lived in the White River region of Missouri, so he built a canoe and floated down the Mahoning River to the Ohio River, and on to the Mississippi River, and finally up the White River into the Ozarks.

While visiting here, he started attending a small, one room log church. One Sunday, when the traveling preacher failed to show up, he was asked to preach. The sermon was so well received, he was asked to be the regular minister. Preaching became his calling.

As a preacher, Harold lived in several areas of the Ozarks. He first lived in White Oak, but was then offered a church near Pierce City. He next moved to Pittsburg, Kansas, to preach, and there he met Frances Long, who had known him at Hiram College. They were later married.

They had three sons, one born in 1901, one in 1902, and

---

3. Harold Bell Wright, *Storyteller to the World*, Lawrence V. Tagg.
4. Ibid.

the third in 1910. In 1903 Harold's first book, "The Printer of Udell's," was published and was moderately successful.

About this time, he again became ill, and had to give up preaching. He and his wife moved back to the Ozarks, staying in a tent at "Inspiration Point," which is now a part of the Shepherd of the Hills Homestead.

Harold got to know the hill people and listened to their many stories. One of the stories inspired the book, "The Shepherd of the Hills." The book was a great success, and immediately put the national spotlight on this backward, isolated region.

In 1960, the Shepherd of the Hills Outdoor Theatre was built near the Inspiration Point site, and every night during the summer season, area people reenact the Shepherd of the Hills story. The play averages over 250,000 spectators a year.

As I look up at the sky full of stars, I realize this is the same view of the night sky that Harold Bell Wright looked up at. And below me is the same Mutton Hollow he wrote about. And off to the west, now covered by darkness, are the same ridges he and his wife Frances watched the sun go over.

I try to imagine the nights back in the early 1900's, as Harold sat alone on a hilltop, the stars filling the vast sky, and the hills totally lost in darkness, with no street lights, yardlights, or neon signs intruding. Just the stars, and the crickets and whippoorwill calling through the night.

And I think about the huge clouds of bats that would circle up out of Marvel Cave at dusk and spend these dark hours crisscrossing the night sky, catching hundreds of tons of insects in a single evening. And at dawn, they would return to the dark recesses of the cave once called the Devil's Den, to sleep through the day.

The cave is located just to the west of where I am now, and I can see the lights of Silver Dollar City, which is located right above it.

Visitors had come to Marvel Cave for many years, so a

few shops were opened near the entrance. These shops have evolved into an 1880's and Victorian Era theme park that now hosts millions of tourists every year.

Around 1959, the same time that Table Rock Dam was completed, four brothers from near Highlandville, Missouri, decided to start playing country music in Branson. The Mabe brothers chose the name "Baldknobbers" for their group, wearing hillbilly type clothes and playing makeshift instruments. Comedy was a mainstay of their act.

They began attracting a following, and other music groups moved into the area. Now, some thirty years later, over twenty music shows with more than 18,000 seats line Highway 76. These country music shows have become so popular that Branson claims the title of "Country Music Show Capital of the World." Along with the local entertainers, most major country music stars perform here during the season.

Summertime in Branson is a hotbed of activity. But for now, at this time of the morning, the town, though brightly lit, is quiet and serene.

I look off into the darkness of the valley to the northeast. Every once in a while the flash of light from a lightning bug reminds me that a very active, hidden nocturnal world is moving all around me.

This early in the morning, most of the fireflies have slowed their activities, but before midnight, the signalling for mates was fairly intense. The males give off a three-tenths of a second flash every five-and-a-half seconds, and then wait for a female to return the signal in two seconds. The male is able to recognize the correct signal from a potential mate.

This flashing, or bioluminescence, is a form of light known as cold light, since no heat is given off. It is created by a mysterious chemical reaction that occurs when certain chemicals in the firefly's abdomen are exposed to oxygen.

This bioluminescence is not unique to fireflies, though. It is found in certain kinds of plants, insects, and marine life. One common form in the Ozarks, besides the firefly, is the luminous fungi, or Foxfire. It grows on wood where the ground is wet. It can give off a blue to green or yellow color. The fungi, *clitocybe illudens*, is also called Jack-O-Lantern.

The eerie glow that the fungus emits has long been associated with the supernatural world. Since foxfire can only be seen at night, many superstitious hill folk have thought is was ghost lights.

Tales of these ghosts, or haints, have passed down from generation to generation, and have undoubtedly been embellished as time has passed.

I look again into the darkness of Mutton Hollow, and recall the Haint of Mutton Hollow in the book, "The Shepherd of the Hills."

These superstitions have strong support in some of the more ardent believers, giving rise to all sorts of potions and incantations to ward off the suspected evils. Many of the earlier doctors dealt with spiritual healing and psychic healing as much, if not more, than they did with the physical sciences.

Quite often this doctoring tied in directly with religion, which has had a strong influence on human life in the Ozarks since this region was first inhabited by man. Since both internal medicine and religion were mysterious, it's no wonder that the medicine man was both doctor and priest.

The Osage Indians believed strongly in Wah-Kon-Tah, the great spirit, as being the overseer of their world, as well as the spiritual world, since they believed that all living things on earth possessed a spirit.

After the white man came into the area and drove the Indians out, Christianity became the dominant belief. Denominations such as Baptist, Church of Christ, Episcopalian, Methodist, Pentecostal, Presbyterian, and Church of God established strong roots in the Ozarks, along with Catholic, Jehovah's Witness, and many congregations that didn't cling to any prescribed denominational teachings.

Out of some of these groups came unique practices, such as foot washings, faith healing, and speaking in tongues. The practices were believed to show one's worthiness, or to make someone worthy enough to have a spiritual relationship with God. These activities are still practiced today.

My mom has always been a source of family history for me, and I remember several of the more colorful stories she's told me about some of the preachers that we've had in the family, most of them living in the Boston Mountains of Arkansas.

A great-grandfather of mine was a Pentecostal preacher who also chewed tobacco. It is said he would preach across the room, stop and spit out the window, and then preach back to the other side. I don't know what he did in the winter when the windows were closed.

One of my other forefathers was also a preacher, but from some of the stories I've heard, I'm not sure just where he drew the line between the physical and spiritual world. It's a familiar story.

I've also read about the old camp meetings that would last for up to two weeks. A family would travel by wagon, carrying enough food and clothes for the entire two weeks, and would camp on the grounds. That sort of religious fervor isn't as common today.

Though brush arbors or tent revivals aren't seen as often as they once were in these hills, there still is the Sunday afternoon baptism at a local swimming hole, followed by a dinner on the grounds, or an all night gospel sing, or a healing service.

On summer nights like this, you can drive down a country road, and hear the driving beat of electric musical instruments coming from open windows of a church or hear the congregation singing a favorite hymn, or shouting and clapping their hands with fervent intensity.

I remember going to a few meetings like this when I was younger. Having been raised fairly conservatively as a Southern Baptist, the clamor of the charismatic services was discomforting, to say the least. Since I'd been conditioned to a religion in which the congregation sat submissively while the preacher controlled the services, the intense involvment of the congregation in these Pentecostal meetings seemed to me to border on anarchy, and I always felt a greater spiritual peace after leaving the church.

I sit down on my platform in the sky and make myself comfortable. The stars shine on as a breeze briefly swirls and then abates. The sound of the crickets, and tree frogs, fills the night. The whippoorwill has become silent.

This is my church. The whippoorwill has finished its beautiful sermon, and the crickets and frogs are singing the invitation. Off in the darkness, from the amen corner of a dark hollow, a dog gives a bark. I let the spirit work.

As I sit in my peaceful world, the brightness of the stars begins to wane, ever so slowly, as the sky gradually takes on the morning light. Through the surrounding darkness, I begin to see the outlines of hills and valleys, trees and glades.

The traffic along the highway is showing a little more activity, but nothing like what is yet to come. A large produce truck passes by below.

These hills are extremely inspiring, and seem to be a magnet for many creative people. Several nationally known authors make this area their home, as well as their base of operations.

There are also internationally known songwriters and performers that were born and raised in these hills, along with several famous actors and actresses, who not only grew up in this region, but also studied their craft here.

Artists can be found painting everything from quick

sketches, characterizations, portraits, nature and wildlife scenes, to decorating saw blades, barn wood, washboards, and even rocks. If it doesn't move, it can be painted. And these artist use many different mediums also, such as oil paint, watercolors, pen and ink, and so on.

Other craftsmen that live here are quilt makers, potters of national prominence, stained glass makers, metal workers, dried flower arrangers, broom makers, woodworkers, which includes world famous wood carvers, clock makers, basket weavers, leather workers, gunsmiths, etc.

If it can be conceived, it can probably be made by one of the artisans of the Ozarks. I've never been in any place that had such a high concentration of creative people in such a small area.

If I go to the Post Office, or to a local cafe or coffee shop, I will probably pass by an actor, or entertainer, artist, author, potter, woodcarver, songwriter, or numerous other craftsmen, some who excel in several areas, who are going about their daily lives with a modest sense of self importance. Some sit and discuss the weather, or how business is going, and all seem fairly content to call the Ozarks home. I wonder what artist or maybe a songwriter is sitting and waiting for the same event that I am at this very minute.

The trees in the valley are beginning to take shape as the world grows steadily lighter. The eastern sky has become a bright blue. A glade off to the north is light enough for me to see the isolated cedars that are scattered around it.

As I look down into the clearing, the shadowy outline of a deer moves from out of the forest. It doesn't seem to be in any hurry to move on to the tree line on the other side.

The whitetail deer, *odocoiles virginianus*, is common in the Ozarks, but it's still enjoyable to be able to watch one move nonchalantly, totally unaware of my presence. The deer feeds on grass, occasionally lifting its head to look toward the valley, or to look around for the most tender shoots, and then it lowers its head again to eat.

There was a time when the whitetail had several predators in this area, but with the disappearance of the wolf, panther, and bear, their main predator is man. Although they are somewhat protected by established hunting seasons, a rifle shot in the night might be the signal that a deer's been spotlighted illegally, and is headed for someone's freezer.

The other main predators in this region are the coyote and bobcat. Coyotes may take a newborn fawn, but adult deer, unless sick or injured, have little to fear.

The bobcat, *felis refa*, is not large enough to bring down a deer, and usually ends up feeding on rodents, rabbits, and birds.

The deer moves to another part of the clearing as the sky continues to brighten.

Birds start moving around in the trees, chattering to one another, as a breeze starts to blow in from the southeast, bringing the sweet smell of summertime with it.

Looking off to the east, I can see a few patches of clouds along the horizon; dark gray against the blue sky.

The breeze that is gently blowing has begun to pick up whisps of fog out of the valleys, and is streaming them slowly up the draws.

I look back at the glade, but the deer is no longer in sight.

The sky is bright blue in the east, but as I look back to the west, its shade darkens. The darker shade of blue makes me stop and I feel a chill. It is such an odd color, one that I will never forget.

One year ago, I was in a local restaurant at about four o'clock in the afternoon. The restaurant was part of a motel complex, complete with swimming pool. I heard a commotion from across the room and saw several customers standing up and looking out. I didn't pay much attention to them until I heard someone ask, "Is he dead?"

I went to the window, and saw a crowd of people standing around a body that was lying at the side of the pool. Everyone was just standing there looking down, so I ran out the door and sprinted to the pool. As I think back, I remember the feeling that I wasn't really moving myself, but as though someone or something else was making me run.

When I got closer, I could hear people yelling, "Somebody, do something," or "I don't know what to do."

It was total chaos. Everyone was in a panic, except the man lying on the deck. He was dead.

I'd learned cardiopulmonary resuscitation, CPR, about nine years earlier, but I'd never used it. But since no one else was doing anything, I felt I had to try something, and went down on my knees beside the body.

At the same instant, a waiter who was just coming to work, only seventeen years old, appeared beside me and asked if I knew CPR. When I told him I did, he said that he did too, and if I would do the breathing, he would do the compressions.

For the next fifteen minutes or so, the world went out of focus for both of us as we went into what can best be described as a state of total concentration, brought on by desperation and panic.

As I looked into the face of the corpse, I was quite shocked by the blue color of the oxygen starved flesh. The color is still vivid in my mind, and in the sky.

As Paul, the young waiter, counted aloud each time he pushed against he man's sternum, I would periodically put my mouth over the lifeless blue mouth and blow, almost oblivious to the undigested food that the man expelled onto my arms, clothes, face and mouth.

All around us the chaos continued as people yelled instructions, or apologized to each other for not being able to help, or cried and screamed.

One elderly little man, partially drunk, with a drink still in his hand, stood over us, yelling, "Clear his mouth, clear his mouth," or do this or do that, followed by a string of oaths. When someone would tell him to be quiet, he would announce, "I'm a retired fireman," and then would curse some more.

One man asked him why he hadn't done something himself, and he admitted he didn't know how, and then continued to yell and curse.

Paul and I ignored the barrage as best we could, focusing every bit of our energies into saving the drowned man's life.

The ordeal seemed to last forever, but finally the man coughed. At first I thought it was just another of the gurgling sounds that the water was making in his chest each time I blew, but I knew better when he took a breath. His color began to return to normal as oxygen-carrying blood once again began to course through his veins.

A passing nurse came upon the scene and I willingly gave up my place and hurried to the pool to wash my face nd arms.

The drunk little man continued to curse and criticize, totally unaware of just how close he was to becoming the recipient of my emotional purging. Thankfully, he reminded me of a small yapping dog. Yapping dogs irritate me sometimes, but I usually pity them because they are yapping out of fear. I realized that the little man was just trying to compensate for feelings of inadequacy, so I just walked away.

A man had just come back to life, and another had just been initiated into manhood, and I had come one step closer to facing that thing that haunts me most - death. So I just couldn't be bothered.

The drowning victim did regain consciousness and spent a week in intensive care where they worked night and day to remove the fluid from his lungs, some of which I helped put there.

I regret that I wasn't able to talk with him about what he had experienced. I've wondered if he was aware of it all, or if it was like being asleep. I've heard accounts of near death experiences, where some say that they saw lights at the end of a tunnel, or were met by deceased friends or relatives. Some even claim to have had out of the body experiences where they watched the drama played out around their lifeless body.

Maybe someday I'll meet the man again and we can talk.

The picture of his lifeless blue face once again comes into my mind, but I quickly look away from the blue sky to the highway down below.

The street lights are still on, but they are of little use since the world has grown light. There are still a few bugs that haven't given up their futile circling, but it will soon end.

The sky in the east is now very bright with a pink hue covering the blue. The clouds are also taking on a reddish cast, signalling that something is getting ready to happen.

The birds are now fully awake, singing and flying around looking for food. Squirrels are running along their limb highways, playing games of tag through the leaves.

I notice one of the street lights turning off automatically. It's getting light enough that the light sensors will start shutting each of them off. Looking down over the area, I watch this slow motion process; one here, then another on a far off hill, then another over on a side street. Since the sensing units on the individual lights obviously aren't closely calibrated, there is no pattern in their shutdown; but finally almost all of them make it. Something is starting to happen in the sky, so I look away.

The color of the clouds is starting to get much brighter as the eastern sky begins to glow with a yellow hue. All around me the world is light enough to see clearly. The trees, the hollows, the glades, and the hills all around.

I look back to the clouds whose edges are getting brighter and brighter in color, quickly turning from a deep red to a reddish orange, bordering on golden. The birds are calling as the breeze seems to pick up a bit, anticipating the coming dawn.

And then, as though turned on by a magical switch, the clouds turn golden, their edges shining like highly polished metal.

The rays from the approaching sun stream up from the horizon, accented by shadows cast by some unknown obstacles on the far side of the hills.

The clouds are now totally brilliant, and their incredible color fills me with awe. The sun's edge is just starting to show above the distant ridges. I watch it for a moment, but as it clears the horizon, the eastern sky explodes in golden light, forcing me to look away. It's sunup in the Ozarks.

This scene has been repeated millions and billions of times throughout the history of this planet, but still I know that this morning is unique. The clouds are shaped differently than they've ever been before, and the sun has shone on the clouds at a different angle, and the atmosphere that the sun's light passes through is made up of a different combination of elements than ever before, making the shade of refracted light a little different than yesterday, or than it will be tomorrow. This is a special day.

The warmth from the sun feels good as I sit facing the huge fire ball while it clears the horizon. All around the hills and ridges are aglow in bright yellow light that throws long shadows across the valleys and down the canyons.

The whisps of steam rising from the draws turn a creamy white in the morning light. The cedars in the glade reflect the light from their eastern side, but the backside still hides in the shadows. The deer has not returned. Patches of gray headed cornflowers grow in the clearings, along with other wildflowers, and catch the morning light.

These cornflowers, like all the flowers of the aster and daisy families are composites. What appears to be a single flower is actually a group of tiny flowers arranged in dense heads. There are 370 native composites and 90 introduced species that grow wild in this region. Mist flowers, white snakeroot, goldenrod, asure aster, cornflowers, butterflyweed, and musk thistle are just a few varieties of the composites that grow in fence rows, along roadsides, and in fields throughout the Ozarks, adding so much to its beauty.

The beautiful sunrise continues to unfold.

Across the valley to the northeast, two turkey vultures, *cathartes auras*, appear, riding along on the wind. They make slow, sweeping circles, constantly scanning the earth for food, which is mostly insects, small mammals or carrion. With their nests secure in trees, or on a cliff shelf, they can be seen flying across Ozark skies any time of the day, in all kinds of weather, the year around.

As I watch, I'm amazed at their ability to find the invisible thermals, and let the rising air flows buoy them up, making the need to flap their wings to retain altitude almost unnecessary. Around and around they soar, the feathers along the edges of their wings constantly being tilted, raised or lowered in what appears to be an automatic, effortless reaction; taking advantage of the laws of aerodynamics, and somehow defying the laws of gravity, while the vulture concentrates on finding a meal. We still have so much to learn.

I decide to stand up, stretching out my legs and moving around to increase the circulation and regain the feeling in my hips. I was sitting down longer than I'd realized. Walking around the edge of the platform, I first look down on the highway and the cars that are beginning to move around. I look past the highway down into Mutton Hollow, and think about the old shepherd and his flock in the book, "The Shepherd of the Hills." Along the horizon above Mutton Hollow rise mountain peaks that are somewhere down in Arkansas.

On to the west stands the office building and entrance to Silver Dollar City, which is over Marvel Cave.

On to the right, at the site where Harold Bell Wright and his family camped, stands the new observation tower that's been built this year.

Following the horizon on to the north, above the glade and to the east, I see the water towers around Forsyth, and the hills beyond near Hercules Glades.

As my eyes squint into the morning sunlight, I can see

Snapp Bald, where the first Baldknobbers met to form their vigilante police force.

On toward the southeast, beyond the highway, the motels, restaurants, swimming pools, gift shops, and music shows, beyond the go-cart tracks and miniature golf courses, beyond the airport at The School of the Ozarks, I see the hills that hold Murder Rocks, and the caves of Alf Bolin, and the fields of Civil War battles and skirmishes.

I'm looking out over the hills that have been crossed by traveling preachers, bringing religion to isolated people; hills that overlook valleys where baptizings still take place in meandering rivers, where the nighttime exposes the flash of the firefly, the call of the whippoorwill, or the cry of the hoot owl, and the eerie glow of foxfire; where people still hold on to some superstitions, that grow in the shadows of the unknown.

And hills that attract artists, writers, sculpters, carvers, singers, actors, and performers of all kinds.

And the hills that I feel hold answers for me. Somewhere here there is a message that will "fire me up," that will unleash my spirit and let me ride on the wind without effort, defying the natural laws of gravity. And that will free me from my fear of death and the unknown.

Somewhere in these hills there is a key to help me unlock the door. Somewhere I will find my inspiration, for this is an inspiring land.

Day Nine
July 14

Brother Versus Brother

I jump at the exploding sound of thunder directly overhead. The ground shakes around me as the echo rolls down the canyon.

In the sky the dark clouds seem to be boiling as the winds toss and swirl the clouds around, just like currents I've seen working in streams on early summer mornings when pollen that has collected on the water is swirled, dipped and pushed all about as it passes through a rapids.

The clouds are churning as the squall line gets closer. I hope that no funnel clouds decide to make a surprise visit.

The wind that's being pushed ahead of the approaching storm sweeps through the trees, twisting and bending the leafy branches, sending a rolling wall of dust, leaves, and dried grasses flying.

The air feels charged, and the smell of rain sends me hurrying for shelter.

The first raindrops send up little puffs of dust from the ground as they slam into the dry soil. The heavier rain quickly follows, dampening the ground completely. The fresh rain has such a wonderful smell.

The first sounds are the rain against the leaves, but that is quickly drowned out by the torrents of rain falling everywhere. The sound is almost deafening. As the gutters begin to fill, a waterfall cascades off the corner of the roof, splashing onto a flat piece of rock.

The sound of the rain reminds me of steaks being cooked on a grill at an afternoon barbecue, but there will be no cookout today.

The water falling from the roof quickly forms a tiny rivulet that begins seeking out a place to go. It snakes its way across the lawn.

The lawn, with the grass evenly trimmed on top, appears

to be level, but as certain areas fill with water, forming miniature reservoirs that overflow into tiny streams that weave their way through the grass, it's easy to see where there are little hills and valleys underneath the foliage. The small streams make their way toward the valley below.

A house sparrow, *passer domesticus*, shows little concern of me as it takes refuge under an overhang of the roof. It hunches down and fluffs up its feathers to stay warm and dry. It has pulled its head up close to its body and, as it looks out at the rain, gives a halfhearted chirp, but doesn't move.

Irregular bursts of wind send sheets of driving rain against the roof, trees, and lawn. The air and ground are getting a much needed cleansing, as the dust and pollen that so quickly builds up in July is being washed away.

Ditches and small streams begin to fill as the run-off from the surrounding land increases.

Another flash of white light makes me cower, even though I feel fairly safe from the millions of volts of electricity that's passing from cloud to cloud in the air above. I stay tense momentarily, until the inevitable crash of thunder comes, once again shaking the ground and echoing off the distant bluffs.

I wonder how earlier peoples came to terms with lightning and thunder storms. I wonder what they thought the incredibly beautiful and dangerous lightning bolts were, and how they interpreted thunder.

Again there is a flash and thunder crashes overhead, its sound rolling down the White River valley.

How many echoes have been heard in these hills? How many waves of sound have slammed against tree, rock or hill? Not just the sound of thunder, or the falling of a tree, or the crashing of rocks from the slowly eroding bluffs, but also man-made sounds. Like the sound of sonic booms that seemed to be everywhere in the 1960's, or the sounds of explosives that blast through the rock at construction sites, or at quarries, or are used in the mining of minerals, or to blow tree stumps out of the ground while clearing new ground.

Then there is the clatter of horses' hooves over shale rocks, and the crash of wagon wheels over a rocky road, the cracking of a buggy whip, the clashing of steel against steel, the recoil of a rifle or musket, and the deafening burst from a cannon which shakes the ground and then echoes down the canyon; man-made thunder.

The Ozarks have experienced much, too much, of this sound, as war came to these hills.

On July 21, 1861, the Battle of Bull Run was fought in Virginia. The very next day, General T.W. Sweeny and 1,200 Union troops stationed at Springfield attacked the Confederate outpost at Forsyth, below Shadow Rock.

A twelve pound Howitzer was used in the assault.

I can only imagine what the locals thought of the echo of thunder on that sunny July day. That sound echoing down the valley would be heard for the next four years.

The Ozarks was one of the major battle fronts of the Civil War and this land would suffer greatly because of it.

The battle at Forsyth, although minor in comparison to what lay ahead, set wheels in motion that wouldn't stop until they wore out, and not a single Ozarkian was unaffected.

Very few people who lived in these hills had a personal interest in the conflict. There weren't many slaves here, and even fewer slave owners. The United States government was far away, and the isolated hill folks pretty much governed themselves.

The conflict, however, became a whirlwind which began to draw everyone in, whether they wanted it to or not. It swept over the land, much like the storm I'm watching today, but with a much different effect.

After the first battle, the Union forces withdrew to Springfield, taking their plunder with them. Their encroachment into Taney County alienated some people who aligned themselves with the Confederacy. The lines of battle were being drawn.

A few weeks later the Battle of Wilson's Creek was fought, and it was a terrible slaughter on both sides.

The Arkansas-Missouri border was the theoretical diving line between the North and South, but no line could be drawn to separate ideologies. There were people who lived on both sides of the state line that supported the Union, and people on both sides who supported the Confederacy. These differences divided neighbors, many of whom were relatives, and even split up households; father against son, brother against brother, joining on opposite sides for whatever reasons.

There were many who wanted to remain neutral, but they quickly found that war doesn't care about what someone wants. It's a storm that moves through the land, and it rolls over anything or anyone that gets in its way. It is an entity unto itself, and it feeds on destruction.

Many of those who sought neutrality suffered more than those who went to fight. They were preyed upon by bushwhackers and often soldiers from both sides.

If a Union or Confederate recruiter came to a man's house trying to get him to join their army, and he refused to join, he was often shot, since it was assumed he was a sympathizer with the other side.

Many families were looted by whichever force was moving through the area, often driving the victims to support or join the other side.

Also, if a family member was known to be fighting for the other side, this led to repercussions for the ones who stayed behind. These punishments came from not only armies, but neighbors, relatives or bushwhackers alike. Many families, hoping to stay together and alive, fled from these hills into Texas, Kansas and Oklahoma.

The Ozarks quickly became a no man's land where lawlessness reigned. Nothing was sacred or safe. As the people, mostly women, children and old men, struggled to survive, they were constantly preyed upon by marauding bands of deserters from both sides, outlaws from Arkansas, Kansas and Oklahoma, the armies themselves, and even formerly law abiding Ozarkians that had fallen prey to others, and turned to looting to survive.

The homes of people who supported the wrong side were sometimes burned, and the families driven off or even killed.

This war, fought by men who supported a certain ideology, or who sought adventure, or joined purely for self-preservation, changed the lives of all who lived in these hills.

I remember the classic "Gone With the Wind," that details the devastation of the war on the southern aristocracy, but I can't help but feel that there was a greater tragedy here.

These were simple people, surviving in a harsh but beautiful land, that had a war, someone else's war forced upon them. They lost fathers, sons, wives, daughters, whole families, homes and land.

Of the 10,000-plus military actions that took place during the Civil War, over 1,000 took place along the Arkansas-Missouri border; the Ozarks.

This area has paid more than its share of dues to that monster; war. Many area men and women have fought, bled, and died paying the ultimate price during the Civil War, the Spanish-American War, World War I, World War II, Korea, Vietnam, and all those secret wars that go unreported. But, into every battle, memories of this beautiful land went along.

The rain continues to fall. Again lightning flashes in a microsecond of time, but the thunder takes longer to arrive. The storm is passing on to the northeast.

Lightning is such a mystery, just one of the many in nature that hasn't yet been fully solved. It is believed that lightning is electricity that passes from one charged cloud to another, or to the ground, the charging caused by various sized particles falling from the clouds, being electrified by friction within the atmosphere.

But regardless of what causes it, it is incredible. Such an uncontrollable, untapped source of power. One lightning bolt is believed to reach one billion volts, and as much as 200,000 amperes. If man could harness that energy, all of our basic energy needs could be easily met.

I watch as the rain diminishes to a light drizzle.

The sparrow signals the passing of the storm by venturing out from its safe haven, flying off through the dripping trees.

The rain has left my world clean and wet, and it's time for me to venture out also.

I make my way to Table Rock Lake, where I sometimes come at night to get an unobstructed view of the night sky, or to watch the moon bounce its light off the open waters.

In the daytime, this lake is just as beautiful, although today the clouds are still hiding the sun. I watch the distant flash of lightning from the storm that is now off across the eastern hills.

The gusts of trailing winds make ripples that fan out over the lake's surface. The rippling patterns develop, swirl, flare out, disappear, and then reappear again, varied and unique, pushed along by the irregular winds.

I watch as the wind works far out across the mile or two of water between me and the distant shore.

Far out there is a flock of waterfowl, too far away to identify, appearing as closely grouped tiny black dots that bob up and down on the waves.

The lake is surrounded by wooded hills, with their lush green foliage occasionally accented by the gaunt skeleton of a tree that's died but hasn't yet yielded its place in the sky.

Through the deciduous trees are woven conifers, mostly red cedar, that remain green the year around, but some of them have succumbed to the July heat, and now reflect a sunburned, rusty hue.

The forests open into small glades where the soil is too

shallow for most trees to set their roots, and only undernourished cedars and small bushes dot the area.

These openings offer opportunity for the smaller plants to flourish, and at this time of the year these glades are still decorated with the colors of blossoms of goatsbeard, elderberry, cornflowers, blazing stars, musk thistles, false dragonheads, common milkweed, columbine, black-eyed susans, and the bright orange butterfly weed. These flowers provide a nice complement to the cacti and assorted grasses that grow in these glades.

In the evenings, deer work their way through these clearings, contentedly grazing on the plants that sprout out of the thinly soiled beds of rock, their hooves clicking against the stone, and their short white tails constantly fanning. Their tails work as a form of communication, as well as to ward off the biting flies that can be relentless.

In the daytime, the glades play host to groundhogs that constantly munch on vegetation as they work to build up necessary stores of fat for the winter.

Rabbits frequent these areas, too, attracting hawks and foxes.

Standing on the shore where the waves crash against the rock shelf beneath me, I look up and see that the clouds are now very high. The upper winds are sweeping the clouds along, giving them a brushed look. A curl here, a flair there, a coiffure in the sky.

Off to the west, just above the distant hills, is a thin line of bright blue sky all along the horizon, as the high pressure is quickly moving in behind the low front that's just moved through. Already it's getting lighter.

The rocks and trees are still wet from the rain. As the wind blows through the timber, drops of water cascade down onto the carpet of dead leaves that cover the ground below, remnants of past summers, waiting to return to the soil.

These miniature showers fall in brief bursts as the wind gusts pass quickly through the trees, here and then gone.

The lake is almost deserted. The usual fishing and pleasure boats that converge on this lake in summer are still secured at the docks where they went to escape the lightning. However, one of the obviously more irresponsible boaters moves his craft up the lake on the far side of the channel. Tempting fate is common to our species.

Looking into the water near the shore, I see a movement near a rock that juts out to my right. A small bluegill, *lepomis macrochirus*, works around the rocks looking for a meal. These little sunfish are prized by fly fishermen for their gamely fight.

They usually feed on insects, mollusks, crayfish, and smaller fish, but as fishermen know, they'll attack almost anything put on the end of a hook, sometimes the bare hook itself.

Since they often school, a great many can be caught at one time. At night, boats can be seen with a lantern light shining to attract the bluegill and crappie, or rather the smaller fish that these sunfish feed on.

One of the bluegill's favorite prey is the shiner, who get its name from its mirror-like sides that reflect light as it turns in the water.

The shiners don't usually have much color, but in the spring, during their mating season, males develop bright color markings. Some get red fins, while others get red stripes. In these waters there are the whitetail, dusky stripe, and the bleeding shiner. Each one is distinct from the other.

Food is plentiful for the many game fish that live here. There are the crappie, goggle-eye, muskie, catfish, bass, paddlefish, trout, and walleye, to name a few, that live in the underwater food chain.

I wonder how it affected the food chain in 1874 when the Ozarks was hit by a plague of grasshoppers. It must have been a feast for the fish and birds, even though it was such a hardship on the people and land animals that were still recovering from the ravages of the war that had ended nine years earlier.

As the wind surges and then grows calm, and then again swirls and tacks it way across the lake's surface, I'm reminded of how the sporadic wind is much like nature's cycles. Feast and then famine. Fire, storm, plague, war and then peace, or overabundance, or survival. All very unpredictable and changing, returning to another cycle. Each time a little different, but also much the same.

This must be a part of Darwin's concept of evolution; the gradual changing. So gradual in fact, it can only be seen after a long period of change.

The little things that cause the changes seem unimportant, such as the water that moves always downward, or the wind moving toward the least resistance, high pressure to low pressure, or electricity moving from charged clouds to uncharged clouds or to the ground. And after the lightning comes the thunder, and after that silence once again comes to the forest and glade, and peace returns to the rock bluffs and stream beds.

I look out across the wide expanse of lake and wonder just where the main channel of the White River ran. I regret not being old enough to have seen it in its freedom; the wilderness not being dotted with motels and resorts, or lake homes, boats, marinas, dams, and all the other trappings of civilization; where deer, bear, panther, bobcat, and eagle could be seen as I float down the pristine river in a flat bottomed boat.

I can see an early morning breakfast cooking in a black cast iron skillet over a driftwood fire, built on a gravel bar in the middle of the stream. The smoke drifting skyward as the bubbling currents play the background for songbirds who fill the cool morning air with their beautiful songs heralding the warm morning sunshine.

Small quick spiders scurry over the polished stones that cover the gravel bar, as they seek food and refuge on this barren island in the middle of the river. Totally peaceful.

The gravel bar holds clues that men have been here

before though, as a pile of broken mussel shells indicates that someone came looking for the pearls of White River. Pearling was common here.

There was some pearl fishing before the Civil War, but the war halted it for a while. However, in 1897, a Dr. Meyers found a fourteen grain, fine luster pearl in a mussel's shell and the pearl mania began.

People came from all over to seek their fortunes. It is reported that a single gravel bar would have as many as 500 men, women, and children, of all colors and social classes, on it.

Some would wade out into the water to gather the mussels, while others opened them. Everyone talked and laughed as they searched for the pearls.

A good day's wage was fifty cents, so this was a great opportunity for the people of this region to make some good money, since the pearls sold for one to two dollars each on the average.

However, some of them offered instant wealth, selling for $100, $500, and one pearl sold for $5,000. It weighed 110 grains.

In 1897, the total value of pearls taken from the river was $11,000, but by 1903 it had increased to $215,000.

All of this pearling left huge piles of mussel shells up and down the river, which offered another kind of wealth. The shells, before the advent of plastic, were used to make buttons, so a whole industry grew here to process the discarded shells.

Most of the locals didn't know or care about the scientific names of the 29 species of mussels found in the White River, so instead of saying *lapsilis ventrilosa*, or *actinonaias carinata*, they called them by names that obviously were derived from their physical characteristics, such as washboards, ladyfingers, butterflies, pimplebacks, pistolgrips, and so on. As long as everyone understood the common language, that was all that was necessary.

As I look out across the water, I wonder why pearling died

off on the river. Maybe the mussels were over fished, or the market for fresh water pearls declined, or maybe the construction of Powersite Dam, which created Lake Taneycomo, played a part. Even still, I wonder if somewhere out there, under all that water of Table Rock Lake, is another 110 grain, fine luster pinkish-colored pearl, just lying there, locked inside a mussel's shell, waiting to be discovered.

In a lot of ways, this lake, this land, and these hills are themselves 110 grain pearls, their secrets locked away, hidden under a rock, or in a stream, or riding on wings high above, or growing in a forest.

Many of these treasures are common, but only because I've not taken the time to find their value. And some of these treasures I will never find, because they are lost to time. They've come and gone with no one to disclose them to me, or no books about them on the library's shelves. It makes me feel sad to think about the loss.

As I stand here, trying to visualize the river that hides beneath this lake, I hear a noise behind me. I turn around in time to see an opossum moving clumsily through the leaves, running on tiny legs, crashing through the undergrowth in its single-minded effort to find safety. This usually nocturnal animal must have been driven from its den by the heavy rain. As it barrels along at an awkward gait, I'm reminded of the common treasures that I overlook.

The opossum, *didelphis virginiana*, from the Greek word *didelphis*, which means double wombed, and *virginiana* meaning Virginia was the first place the white man observed the animal. However, the common name opossum was taken from the Algonquin Indian word, apasum.

These small marsupials, hold overs from an earlier period, have run head on into the twentieth century. Their carcasses litter the highways as these small mammals, whose programmed defenses don't include avoiding automobiles, run across roadways into blinding headlights, and often are killed.

But just what is this animal all about? The opossum has been a food source for the earlier peoples of this region, as well as for dogs, foxes, coyotes, bobcats, great horned owls, bear, panthers, etc. It has also been a source of furs.

They are highly prolific animals. The female has a double cloeca that can be found in the rectal orifice, and the male has evolved complimentary genetalia, having a forked penis to service the two separate oviducts.

Anywhere from twenty to fifty eggs are released during each mating. There is only a thirteen day gestation period after the mating. Usually about twenty tiny babies, each smaller than a honeybee, are born at the same time, emerging from a temporary opening called the false vaginal canal, which connects with both wombs.

These tiny babies haven't fully developed their hind feet, but do have fully developed front legs and hands that they must use to climb up the coarse body hair of their mother to the pouch.

There are thirteen teats in the pouch, twelve arranged in a horseshoe shape with one extra in the center. Since each baby attaches to a nipple and stays there for four to five weeks, only thirteen of the babies can survive.

The babies' eyes open after two months, when they've reached the size of mice. They can be seen in a group, riding on their mother's back until they are three months of age. After that, they're able to go out on their own.

This animal, the opossum, often regarded as a dumb, ugly animal with a long snout and over forty razor sharp teeth, and who hisses loudly when threatened, has evolved into a highly efficient creature that serves its purpose well in the natural order. It is another pearl, and this land is full of pearls.

The light in the west is getting brighter as the high cloud cover is giving way to the blue sky.

As I stand on the shore, the July sun's light finally breaks through the clouds, and immediately I feel its heat. It reflects brightly off the glistening water, forcing me to cover my eyes. I look away.

I decide to start walking back toward the east, and as I do, I see the dark clouds of the earlier storm that have moved off to the northeast. The bright sunshine all around me makes the supersaturated clouds appear even more dark and formidable looking than before.

As the sunlight reaches those clouds, their moisture acts as a prism, refracting the sun's white light into all of its color components, making a rainbow, unbroken end to end; a glowing, colored arch, with not one, but two, pots of gold at the ends, and both hidden somewhere in these beautiful hills.

There it is, the rainbow; the biblical promise that there'll be no more rains that last for forty days and forty nights, no more floods to cover the earth, destroying all but the chosen few.

Looking at the dam, I see man's promise of no more floods on the White River. Even so, high in the sky is a lighted promise also.

Here in this land, the Ozark mountains, where so much has happened, it's true that nature has flexed her many muscles, and natural disasters have followed. But I believe that man-made disasters have been just as bad, or worse.

This place, which at times has been ruled by lawlessness, paid a terrible price to the god of war who pitted brother against brother, now has a beautiful rainbow draped across its sky. The promise.

I try to imagine what a difference it would have made to this region if the promise had been no more war.

Day Ten
August 17

Trials by Fire

It's sure a hot one today!

Perspiration trickles down my face and the back of my neck. My arms, chest, back, and legs are also wet with sweat, even though I sit motionless in the shade, a few feet away from Table Rock Lake.

The temperature is over 100 degrees again today; the third day in a row. This high pressure area is sitting over the central United States, and there is little hope of relief for the rest of the week. The heat shelters up in Springfield have opened, offering refuge for the elderly or people with small children. Everyone seems to be trying to find ways to stay as cool as possible.

The lake is packed with boats and swimmers.

Without a hint of a breeze, the air feels thick and heavy. The leaves on the trees that cover the hills around the lake look wilted and slightly browned. Not many creatures are moving around today, except for the bothersome fly that resists almost every attempt to drive it away, landing and holding on, or walking around, flying off only far enough to avoid being hit by a hand or towel, and then immediately landing again.

This aggravation only causes me to exert more energy than I want to, and makes me sweat even more, which will attract other flies.

Finally I decide to cool off by taking a dip in the water. The rocks and sand that line the shore are hot, and burn the soles of my feet as I hurry to the water. My steps are somewhat exaggerated as I quickly pull up each foot from the burning rocks, almost hopping along.

The sun bares down on my shoulders and back as I wade into the water. The water near the lake's edge is almost too hot. Except for the sun on my skin, the water actually feels warmer than the air around me. It begins to feel cooler as I get out to the deeper water.

In one motion I go under, only staying down long enough to get thoroughly drenched, and then coming back up, wiping the water from my face and hair. As I start back toward the shore my legs fight against the resisting water. The rocks on the lake's bottom feel sharp as they ambush my tender feet. I get out and hurry back across the hot beach to my place in the shade.

The air feels much cooler now as my dripping body dries. The evaporation process lasts for a little while, but then I notice I'm again starting to sweat, and another fly begins to buzz around, checking me out.

I feel lethargic and drained today, but I'm not alone. The beach area is dotted with people who are seeking relief from the heat. Some are sunbathing while lying on half submerged lawn chairs, or floating on air mattresses, others are swimming, or like me, are sitting around in the shade.

Every once in a while one of the sitters or sunbathers will venture out into the water to cool down.

Near the swimming area, pleasure boats of different descriptions are anchored, and people dive from the decks, or just sit around under awnings.

Everywhere there are coolers and other containers filled with cold liquids. The sun continues to assault the earth, and the flies are having a field day. Swimming holes all over the Ozarks are undoubtedly packed today.

For every person who has found the water, there are hundreds more sitting in front of fans or air conditioners, trying to escape the reality of this summer's heat. The sounds of whining electric motors fill the neighborhoods as the window fans strain to move the heavy air, and the air conditioning units work to cool the air inside of houses whose doors and windows are closed up tight to keep the cool in and the oppressive heat out. Small fortresses under siege.

The power stations at the area's dams are constantly running to take care of the increased electrical demands. Warnings periodically appear on television broadcasts or are announced on the radio to remind electrical users that the local power system is reaching maximum usage, and this peak demand is forcing the utility company to buy electricity from other producers in their network, thus raising the costs. For most, the extra cost is a small price to pay for the relief it brings.

This constant generation is also causing lake levels to drop, since many of the creeks and streams that feed into the lake are very low, or even dried up. There hasn't been a good measurable rain for about a month. The lawns and fields are parched and brown.

The bumper to bumper traffic is still heavy on Highway 76, but many of the tourists are confining their activities to mostly the morning and evening hours. During the hottest part of the day they stay inside the air conditioned motel rooms, music show matinees, or wander around in cool gift shops and malls. Some go to the water parks to cool off.

The drivers that do get out on the road find that the slow pace of the traffic and the extreme heat may take their toll. Now and then a stalled, overheated automobile, with its hood up and clouds of steam rolling, sits in a parking lot or unmoving on the road. Wrecker drivers and mechanics are taking advantage of the bonanza.

Tempers are becoming shorter and blood pressures are rising as the slow moving cars can be more like ovens than transportation. This is the time of year when everyone and everything has an increased combustibility. One spark and it can all explode.

An example of that occurred in Branson just over 75 years ago. On a hot August day in 1912, a wood burning kitchen stove apparently overheated and ignited the Commercial Street Hotel. The fire quickly spread as it was driven by dry winds, and no one could stop it.

An older gentleman told me of how he had witnessed the fire when he was young. He talked about the firestorm that swept over the downtown business district in a very short time, the heat and smoke being unbelievable.

Of the 24 businesses in Branson, twenty were totally destroyed. All that remained were a few brick walls and charred cinders.

The four buildings that survived were a bank, a lumberyard, a saloon, and livery stable. That was apparently enough for survival, because the town was rebuilt, and exactly one year later the local people announced the rebirth. But less than two months later, in October, 1913, another fire started and burned six of the newly constructed buildings.

As hot and dry as it is today, I can see why a fire would be hard to control. I'm sure that fire spotters from the forest service are busy monitoring every puff of smoke that rises up through the trees.

Public service announcements have asked people to limit their burning, and hopefully everyone will use common sense. But still, the sight of smoke from a barbecue grill, or a controlled burn in a bulldozed area brings the authorities to a heightened state of alert.

It has been speculated by some that this extremely hot weather may be due to the depletion of the ozone layer in our upper atmosphere, which acts to filter out harmful solar radiation.

Others believe the heat wave may be a result of cyclical sunspot activity, since we are entering a very active time, with the solar storms being much more pronounced. I'm not sure just how these solar disturbances affect our weather, though. It might be somehow affected by the increased magnetic activity, since these storms are magnetic in nature.

The energy that's involved in one of these flares is tremendous, spreading over the sun's surface at 1,000 kilometers per second for distances of 500,000 kilometers.

When this happens, burning gasses are ejected out from the sun's surface at over 100 kilometers per second.

These fountains are visible using special equipment, and the sight of burning gasses being shot into space hundreds and thousands of miles is unbelievable.

The energy expended by one solar flare is greater than all of the energy that could be used on the earth for nine million years. There wouldn't be any need for a peak alert if we could learn how to draw from that energy source. Our dams could take a vacation.

It's believed that this sunspot activity, which usually increases for eleven years, is going to be one of the most active periods that has been recorded. This may cause a severe change in the weather, and we might be facing a long term drought.

One of the worst droughts in this area was in 1930. That August the temperature stayed above 110 degrees for quite a while. Wells dried up, and there was very little food for humans or livestock.

It was so bad in this region, President Hoover asked the Red Cross to help out. However, the organization couldn't do a whole lot, because it, like the government during those years of the Great Depression, just didn't have the resources. I'm glad I wasn't here then.

I do remember the drought of 1980, though. It wasn't anything like the 1930 drought, but the extreme heat did go on for weeks. The lake levels dropped drastically.

The lake's level is starting to get low again, and more and more shore line is visible between the trees and the water, as air conditioners continue to run.

I wonder what it was like to endure the heat of August before the days of electricity. No air conditioning, no electric fans, no running water, no refrigeration, no ice cold drinks in the cooler. None of the many things we take for granted in the modern day Ozarks.

All of those days of unrelenting heat and those long restless nights, so sultry that sleep becomes impossible;

tossing and turning on bed clothes wet from sweat. Hot! Too hot! With little or no escape, only tolerance.

But that was the way of life for the people of this area, who endured much to make these hills their home.

I can imagine a small log cabin setting on the side of a hill, it being only big enough to provide basic shelter for a struggling family, who eked out an existence from the land, as their brood continued to increase and grow.

Out back stood an outhouse made of slab wood. In the front yard, an old cast iron pot hung from a tripod made of logs. Underneath the pot was a pile of partially burned wood, the fire being restarted when clothes needed to be boiled, or when soap needed to be made by rendering fat and combining that with lye. The pot was also used to boil water for pouring over a freshly killed hog, to make the hair removal easier.

The thought of a hill woman standing over a boiling pot in this kind of heat is more than I can handle. I reach into my cooler for a can of ice cold soda.

The women that have repopulated these hills for generations have proven that they are by no means the weaker sex. These females often married around the age of thirteen or fourteen, not completely through puberty, and usually began bearing children almost immediately.

They were responsible for cooking, cleaning, spinning, sewing, foraging for herbs and foodstuffs, plowing and planting and harvesting, canning, helping with the butchering, dressing game, smoking and salting the meat, milking, mothering, doctoring, and all the rest that goes along with being a woman. Their lives were hard, but they accepted their lot in life with resolve.

Though life for most of the women in the Ozarks was hard, at times it could get even harder. For many of them, they at least had a man around who could help provide for the family, and help shoulder some of the responsibilities. But when the man left, or died, the whole burden fell on the woman.

Many Ozarks women lost husbands during the Civil War, some in battle, some to bushwhackers, and some to disease. But in this untamed land, others were killed when someone got caught up in the heat of passion.

There was one night, near Chadwick in Christian County, when a family was all but destroyed by just such a situation. The Taney County Baldknobbers, led by Captain Kinney, had been publicly disbanded, but the Baldknobbers in Christian County, a separate group led by "Bull Creek Dave" Walker, continued to "law" their county. They gathered one night in March to go and destroy some whiskey that belonged to a moonshiner called "Bucky Bill." Several men met, but when no information on the location of the whiskey was forthcoming, the raid was cancelled, and the group decided to adjourn for the night.

On their way home, some of the younger men, one of them the son of the group's leader, got ahead of the others, and as they passed the cabin of a man who had opposed the Baldknobbers, they decided to let off a little steam by teaching him and his family a lesson.

The situation quickly got out of hand, and when the shooting finally stopped, the old man had been seriously hurt, and his son and son-in-law had been killed. The elderly Mrs. Edens had had a tremendous burden put on her shoulders.

The irate citizens of the county demanded that the offenders be brought to justice, and thus began the biggest trial in Ozarks history.

One of the Baldknobbers that had been identified was quickly arrested. In order to save himself, he gave the names of all the others that had been at the meeting. Most of them were rounded up, but a few had left the area.

The jail at Ozark, Missouri, wasn't big enough to house them all so they were kept on the second floor of the Odd Fellows Hall, chained and manacled together.

A grand jury was impaneled and when its work was

completed, eighty Baldknobbers were charged with some 250 counts, ranging from whippings, intimidations, and pouring out whiskey, to murder.

A few of the men were transferred to the Springfield jail for safekeeping. While they were in the Greene County facility, a new jail was being built in Ozark.

William Walker, the son of the Baldknobber's leader, was one of the men who had been involved in the murders at the Edens' cabin, but he had fled to relatives in Arkansas to evade capture. He was tricked, by the brother of one of the other Baldknobbers who wanted to help his brother get leniency, into coming back into Missouri in order to board a train at West Plains, and escape out of the area. In West Plains, they were arrested by lawmen who were in on the scheme, and young Walker was returned to face trial.

The trials began in August, 1887. I can only imagine how uncomfortable it must have been to be sitting or standing in the throngs of people that jammed the courthouse and the square. The families of the arrested Baldknobbers had come in wagons, and had set up camp around the courthouse. Reporters from all over had converged on the town, filling every hotel room and even some private homes.

On the first day, nine pled guilty to lesser crimes and some of the charges were dropped. Two days later, fifteen more entered guilty pleas for unlawful assembly.

One of the nine turned state's evidence, and the charges against him were dropped. One of the remaining eight was so young, the judge gave him his freedom on a $1,000 bond. Three of the men were given prison sentences. C.O. Simmons, a preacher, was given twelve years, and the other two were given 21 years to serve.

The remaining four were sentenced to hang, their execution set for May of 1888. However, appeals were forthcoming, which delayed the punishment.

During this delay, John and Wiley Mathews escaped, but John, the father, was recaptured. His son was never caught.

The appeals dragged on, but their time finally came in May of 1889. "Bull Creek Dave" Walker, his son William Walker, and John Mathews were hanged. John Mathews died quickly, but the Walkers both fell too low, hitting the ground, which prolonged their deaths. Dave was pulled back up, but his son had to be rehanged. After 35 minutes, it was over. And after two years and two months, the crimes against Mrs. Edens' family had been avenged. But nothing could avenge the burden that had been put on her.

August, 1887, was the beginning of the trial for the Christian County Baldknobbers, but August, 1888, was the last trial of another Baldknobber. Captain Kinney, the founder and leader of the disbanded Taney County Baldknobbers, got into an argument with an old adversary, and was shot to death. There are varied accounts of the incident, but his killer was acquitted.

The captain was buried on his farm, which now lies somewhere beneath the waters of Lake Taneycomo.

These men died leaving behind their devoted wives to struggle and raise their children alone.

Not nearly enough has been put into the history books giving credit to the strength and determination of the women of the Ozarks, who have endured so much and contributed so much to this area.

The sound of someone's radio blaring music brings me back to the present. A song about passion echoes across the water.

I look out and watch boats as they pull skiers across the lake's surface. Skimming across the water looks like an excellent way to escape the heat, with the fine spray of water kicked up by the skis. Boats are moving all around the lake. Off along the distant shoreline pass two sailboats, but their sails are hanging limp in the motionless air. They must be using standby engines to move along.

I feel another fly on my leg and reach to swat at it, when I notice it's not a fly at all, but a tick. American dog ticks, *dermacentor variabilis*, are common around here. They really aren't insects, as many believe, but are acarina, members of the arachnida family.

These creatures usually feed on blood only three or four times in their lives, when they need it to help with their development. When they first hatch out of their eggs, they crawl up on leaves and plants, and wait for a host to come by. They can survive eleven months as a larva without eating, so they wait patiently.

They can tell when a host is near by the smell of butyric acid, which is given off by all mammals. If a host comes close enough, the ticks attach themselves to the skin and feed.

After getting their fill, they drop off and molt. A larva has only six legs, but when it molts into a nymph, it has eight. It then feeds again and molts into an adult. The nymph can go six months without feeding, so sometimes it will hibernate before becoming an adult, or it will change into an adult first, and then hibernate.

The adults mate in the spring, while the female is attached to a host. The male dies immediately after mating, but the female falls off to the ground where she lays her 3,000 to 6,000 eggs that will hatch in two weeks, and then she dies also.

The nymphs and adults spend the winter in moist leaf litter, which makes the Ozarks a perfect place for them to thrive.

Early in the spring many Ozarkers burn off brushy areas hoping to eliminate the ticks, but this is really ineffective. If the leaves are dry enough to burn then the ticks have probably already died, since they need moisture to survive. And only one pair of ticks is necessary to repopulate an entire area, having several thousand babies at once. Also, other ticks are constantly being brought in on birds, wild animals, and livestock.

Many acarina carry various kinds of diseases, the main one now being lyme disease, which can be fatal, so I pull the tick off and study it for just a moment. This one has eight legs, but its abdomen isn't very wide at the back, which indicates it's still a nymph. I send it flying.

Ticks aren't the only pests crawling around in the woods. There are also chiggers, which are a form of mite, that also need to feed on blood. The young attach to the skin, rather than bore into the skin as some believe, and feed before finally dropping off. Adult chiggers don't feed on a host, but only on decaying organic matter. These mites are only the size of a pin's point, and it's very difficult to see them, but they go out of their way to let you know they're there.

As much as I dislike both ticks and chiggers, I realize I'm going to have to get used to them, since there are over 500,000 species of the two on this planet, all hiding somewhere among the leaves.

I look out over the tree covered hills, and see that many of the leaves have lost their bright green luster. The red cedars look scorched as they take on their rusty tint, looking almost as if they are dying. Many of the grasses in the glades have turned a pale yellow, showing no signs of life.

The only blossoms that survive in this heat are the common milkweed, blazing star, musk thistle, black-eyed susan, butterfly weed, false dragonhead, and cornflowers, but even these flowers have lost their glow.

This is the time of year that plants stop their rapid growth, and do their best to survive. The hay fields are drying up, and I doubt that many of the area farmers will get another cutting of alfalfa or fescue.

It's during the days and nights of summer that young men and women earn money by hauling hay from the fields to the barns. But on these "dog days," they're probably out here on the lake, or swinging on a rope out over the water of a local swimming hole.

In this heat, no one could stand being out in the broiling sun "bucking" hay bales, or baking inside a metal roofed barn, trying to fight off swarms of wasps. And besides that, the heat generated by newly baled hay, along with this hot, dry weather, would create a real fire hazard. More than one barn has caught fire due to spontaneous combustion.

The thought of "bucking" hay bales onto the back of a flatbed truck brings back memories. The heat coming off the ground, and the heat from the truck's engine, along with the clouds of exhaust fumes, were stifling. As the sun burned our faces, necks, shoulders, arms, and bare backs, the dust and chaff from the bales would blow back into our faces and stick to our sweating bodies. The chaff itched and burned our eyes, necks, underarms, and anywhere there was movement.

Blisters were quickly worn on our hands, mostly on the inside of fingers, and along the upper part of the palms, caused by picking up bale after bale by the two strands of baling twine wrapped around each one by the baling machine.

As the bales were muscled up onto the truck's bed, the stubbly hay scratched the thigh as it was "bucked" up, and scratched the backs of the forearms as it was pushed on up.

The long days and nights of hay hauling usually ended with the crew going for a refreshing swim in a local creek, usually after dark, and usually sans clothing; skinnydipping.

Today the fields stand empty.

Off over a distant hill, I watch as a small airplane makes a slow circle, its white wings glistening in the sun. It flies straight for a short distance, and then makes another slow circle. It might be someone who is learning to fly, practicing turns, or it might also be a law enforcement officer looking for hidden marijuana patches.

The Ozarks, with its isolated hills and valleys, has always been an excellent place for people who seek seclusion. Many just enjoy the peace and quiet of remote areas, but others prefer the advantage it affords them to escape detection by the law.

Today the stories and songs about making moonshine

are engaging, and glamorize an illegal, unglamorous activity.

In the movies, the moonshiner is often portrayed as a "good ole boy," just trying to survive by supplying a much needed product to the community at large, while bungling, inept lawmen were always lurking around trying to bring these basically good, though a little misguided, citizens to their end. But few things are as they are in the movies.

Moonshine making was one of the things the Scottish and Irish immigrants brought with them to these hills. Alcohol was important in the lives of many hill people, since it was used as a form of medicine by adding it to all sorts of concoctions to treat such things as arthritis, asthma, colds, colic, coughs, croup, toothache, headache, dysentery, pneumonia, rheumatism, and even gallbladder troubles.

One of the things that affected the quality of the homemade alcohol was greed. When the emphasis changed from the making of a good product to the making of a profit, the quality decreased, and it became a much more dangerous brew since short cuts were taken and substitute ingredients were used. Bad moonshine has seriously hurt or killed many an unsuspecting user.

In order to avoid detection, moonshiners used all sorts of tricks to guarantee the secrecy of their still's location. Log sheds, covered with evergreen branches were used, or living saplings were bent over to make a concealment, complete with growing leaves, or the still was built in a ravine and covered with branches, or it was built in a cave and the opening was hidden, or a hole was dug into the earth, the still built inside it and the top camouflaged.

Cold, running water is needed in moonshine making, so it was piped to the site. Many different methods were used to conceal the smoke from the fire, and the smell that came from the whiskey.

When the corn and malt were to be ground up to make the mash and the new beer, it had to be done by a miller who could be trusted not to alert the authorities.

And when the "shine" was finally made, the bootlegger had to use extreme craftiness to get past the law undetected; everything from painting the inside of the jars white to make it look like milk to the building of false bottoms in trucks and cars to hide the liquor.

The making of moonshine isn't as common as it once was, but I know people who swear they could get some pretty easily. They say they know some fellow just over at such and such a place, over near so and so creek, that makes moonshine for $25 a gallon. With the availability of safer, less expensive, government regulated alcohol, I don't really understand why anyone would bother.

Since the market for the illegal booze is small, many of the would-be moonshiners have turned to other illegal endeavors to make money. The first being the growing and cultivation of marijuana, *cannabis sativa*, also known as hemp, which is used to make ropes. But that's not what makes it illegal.

The leaves and stems of the plant contain a chemical, tetrahydrocannibol, or better known as THC, which causes a mild euphoria when smoked, chewed, eaten, or made into a tea. It also causes distortions in the perception of time and space. In heavier doses, it can cause hallucinations, anxiety, depression, paranoia, and forms of psychoses lasting four to six hours. The resin, cannabin, is made into hashish.

Marijuana is a plant native to Missouri, so it grows well in these hills, but unlike the local variety, which isn't very potent and is called "ditchweed" by users, the marijuana being grown for profit may be one of several imported varieties which often come from tropical jungles such as Thailand, Jamaica, Columbia, Mexico, Hawaii, or Panama.

Also, the growing skills of these producers has become so sophisticated, they can increase the potency of a plant by merely pruning it a certain way, or by curing it under certain conditions, or by harvesting it at a certain time.

There has been a whole subculture grow up around the raising of this plant which can bring as much as $100 an ounce.

Every summer the war between the law enforcement community and the "pot" growers seems to peak at this time of the year, because it's nearly harvest time.

Airplanes and helicopters, along with governmental surveillance satellites that fly high above the Ozarks, search forests and corn fields for hidden patches of the illegal weeds. The scenes of raids of houses and farms, and the burning of huge piles of the confiscated marijuana, is a common site in the newspapers or on the evening television news.

However, there is a new problem for law enforcement officials in these hills. It is the making of illegal methamphetamines in makeshift labs. Methamphetamines (d-Desoxyephedrine) is a stimulant, "speed," that increases energy and gives a sense of well-being. It also increases the heart rate and blood pressure. People who use it quickly develop a tolerance for it, requiring more and more to get the same "buzz."

Any kind of building can be used, whether it's a shed, barn, or garage, to conceal the labs that house the highly explosive chemicals that are transformed into highly addictive drugs. And like the latter day moonshiners, the people involved in making "meth" are in it for the large amounts of money to be made, caring little about the quality of the product, or the welfare of the eventual user.

Although there has been an ongoing battle between the "revenuers" and the "moonshiners," the fight between law enforcement and the drug dealers has greatly escalated, with the weapons of this war being some of the most sophisticated destructive arms that our modern technology has devised.

These "Dukes of Hazard" are extremely dangerous.

The plane continues to circle in the distant sky. As I

watch it, I think about how futile many air searches are. If the pilot does spot something, what are the odds that anyone will ever be caught? And if they are caught, what are the chances that the prosecutors will get a conviction?

It seems that lawmen are often fighting the war with their hands tied. Ironically, that's the same situation that caused the formation of the Baldknobbers a little over 100 years ago. They banded together to try to bring law and order to a land that had lost control of the law.

Sometimes it seems we have lost control of the law, and the only people protected by it are the criminals.

I wonder if somewhere in these hills people are meeting, talking about taking over law enforcement themselves, and organizing their own group of vigilantes.

In a lot of ways, I would have to give my silent support, but I've also seen the corruption and abuses that come out of these organizations when people who feel they are powerless organize and suddenly find themselves with power. Power does corrupt! And this land would probably be involved in yet another trial.

The sweat runs down my face and down the middle of my chest. This heat is getting to me again, so it's time to head back into the water.

I know that one of these days this heat will end, and the Ozarks will return to more normal conditions. But for now, I take quick, exaggerated steps as the hot rocks and sand burn the soles of my feet.

Day Eleven
September 15

In the Beginning

The sound of water running in Long Creek is very soothing as I sit near the campfire and watch an occasional spark fly up into the cool September night.

It's been too long since I last spent the night here in Hercules Glades, and this is a perfect night for camping, with a hint of autumn in the air.

The fire hisses and crackles as moisture escapes from the burning limbs. The flames flicker and dance, throwing shadows around the camp that sits in a peaceful meadow close to the middle of this wilderness area.

Hercules Glades is one of the best kept secrets in Ozark Mountain Country. It is made up of a 12,315 acre parcel, located about twenty miles east of Forsyth, which was declared a protected wilderness area in 1976. It is interlaced with many hiking trails that pass through some of the most beautiful and unique scenery the Ozarks has to offer.

The geography of the glades is such that part of it is oak and hickory forests which are interspersed with undernourished cedar trees. The rocky trails take you from the thick forests into open glades where only cedars and prairie grasses grow, along with an occasional cactus, making these areas resemble a desert region. The glades here support life forms not found in other areas of the Ozarks.

Some of the unusual grasses found here are Indian grass, switch grass, big blue stem, little blue stem, prairie dropseed, and side oats gama.

Also, trees such as fringe tree, smoke tree, supple jack, and blue ash flourish.

According to records, there are 39 different species of mammals found here, along with 29 species of fish, 92 species of birds, 34 species of reptiles, and 17 different kinds of amphibians.

About 169 years ago, an explorer and writer by the name of Henry Rowe Schoolcraft came to the glades, and wrote his account of the experience.

Around 1933, there were several homesites in the glades area when the U.S. Government started buying up acreage. Now that the area is no longer populated by people, and the buildings have been removed, and the roads closed, the glades are returning to the way they were when Schoolcraft came here, except that the wolf, bison, elk, mountain lion, and black bear are absent.

However, the collard lizard, or mountain boomer, along with the roadrunner, which are generally found in the southwestern United States, can both be found here.

Native wildlife is also found in abundance. Earlier in the afternoon a wild turkey flew over my campsite from somewhere up on the hill to the northeast, quickly disappearing into the brushy meadow beyond the creek.

The eastern wild turkey, *meleagris gallopava*, was nearly chosen to be our national bird, instead of the bald eagle. If Benjamin Franklin's suggestion had been accepted, they would have been, and one of America's most popular game birds would have been protected. Thanksgiving would have a much different look, with another main course completing the traditional table. But it might have also sealed the fate of the bald eagle. There probably wouldn't have been a Bald Eagle Protection Act of 1940.

Turkeys are native to America, but they got their name due to an odd set of circumstances. When the Spanish Consquistadors came to America, they found the birds in abundance. They took some back to Spain with them around 1500, where they were called "turkey fowl," because they resembled another kind of bird. The turkey was domesticated in Europe, and later brought back to the new world by English settlers. The name turkey was applied to the whole species.

The domestic turkey, though resembling its wild relatives, is much larger in size, reaching as much as fifty pounds, whereas the wild turkey rarely exceeds seventeen pounds. The domestics have more caruncles, which is the bumpy skin that covers the head and neck. Also, it has a large wattle that hangs from its throat, and a longer snood, the skin that hangs from its beak. But even with its larger size, the domestic has a smaller brain.

Domestic males gobble the year around, but the wild males gobble only during mating season, which is early in the spring.

Usually the tom turkeys, along with one in twenty females, grow what are known as beards. It's a long black tuft that resembles hair, and hangs from the middle of the breast. But it isn't really hair, it's modified feathers. These beards usually grow four to five inches a year, and may reach twelve inches in length. It's not a very accurate way to measure a bird's age, however. It would be more accurate to guess a male's age by the length and shape of his spurs, which grow half an inch per year.

At the end of one year, the spurs are rounded on the ends. At two years, the spurs are blunt. But at three years they are sharp. And at four years of age, they are very sharp.

Although domestic turkeys are too heavy to fly, the wild ones can, sometimes reaching speeds of up to fifty miles per hour for short distances. The bird is such a strong flyer, it can actually take off straight up.

When the settlers first came to America, there were about ten million turkeys here, but over-hunting and destruction of habitat took their numbers down to a very few by 1920. But with the help of strong conservation efforts, the turkey is making a comeback.

The Ozarks boasts of a healthy turkey population, with some being trapped and shipped to other parts of the country for restocking those areas.

In the spring, the courting rituals of the turkey are

spectacular. All winter the females and males live apart, but in the spring they join together in flocks, and the forest comes alive with the sound of clucking hens and gobbling toms.

At dawn the toms put on brilliant displays, spreading their tails peacock fashion, and scraping their wings on the ground. At the same time, they throw their chests out and rest their heads back on their shoulders, as they slowly turn and parade around.

These displays are sometimes interrupted as males begin to fight, trying to reestablish their social positions in the flock, since only the dominant males are allowed to fertilize the females.

When a female is ready to mate, she lays down and allows the male to mount her. Before fertilization takes place, the male does a form of posturing dance above her. The reason for this behavior is not quite understood.

Each time a female is fertilized, she goes off to her nest to lay a single egg, until her clutch of eight to fifteen eggs is complete.

After the females are finished laying, they begin to sit on their nests, incubating the eggs, and leave the males to display for themselves. Finally the males leave, and the job of hatching and raising the poults is left to the females.

The female incubates the eggs for about 28 days. After the babies hatch, they quickly learn to follow their mother, who keeps them on the move, foraging mostly for insects, usually grasshoppers, which provide protein for their rapid growth. These poults are extremely vulnerable to predators, with only about half of the brood making it to autumn, when they are able to fly like the adults.

Besides man, the turkey's major predator is the red fox, *vulpes vulpes*, which is common in the Ozarks, living on the abundance of mice, rabbits, eggs, fruit, birds, and carrion. The fox only reaches about fifteen pounds in weight, but is an aggressive hunter.

I've seen these reddish-brown hunters trotting through

the woods on winter days, searching for a meal, their long, bushy, white-tipped tail catching the sunlight and looking much like a flame. The fox's coat is so beautiful, I understand why it's so valued in the fur industry.

The turkey that flew over my camp earlier may have been escaping a near tragedy with a fox; a fox with a fiery tail.

I lean back and look up, catching the light of a few of the brighter stars. The stars won't be shining very brightly tonight because the moon is full, although it will be a while before it makes its appearance over the hill to the northeast.

As I look up, I again feel the chill that comes over me each time I face my insignificance. The universe is so vast, so awesome in its scope, that I will never see much of it, only view a tiny portion of it in the night sky. Lights, so very, very far away.

Not far from camp comes the sound of a small crashing thud, and then silence. It sounded like a walnut falling. This time of year they fall periodically day and night. Sometimes, when the wind blows, a shower of the round, green orbs fall and bounce around, often looking like billiard balls as they strike other walnuts on the ground. It can be dangerous to be too near a tree in one of these downpours. But tonight there isn't any wind, so only the one nut falls, and then silence.

The walnuts are a cash crop in the Ozarks, with whole families gathering the nuts along roadways, in fields, or deep in the woods; anywhere a black walnut tree grows.

Loud, clanking machines that remove the green hulls from the walnuts are set up in different locales, and the nuts are hulled and purchased by weight.

If you don't want to sell your walnuts, you might pay the operator to hull them for you, or just put them in your driveway at home and let the family car do the job.

After the hulled walnuts have dried, they are cracked and eaten, or made into pies, candy, cakes, and many other treats.

Besides black walnuts, these hills also produce hazelnuts, hickory nuts, and butternuts (white walnuts).

I remember spending long hours as a kid, sitting and smashing walnuts with a hammer on the concrete porch, saving some nutmeats in a cup for one of Mom's recipes, and eating the rest. An infrequently smashed finger, or biting down on a piece of hard nutshell, was a small price to pay for the "goodies." I pull a bag of trail mix out of my pack and munch.

The low call of a nightbird through the trees sounds forlorn. The cool night air causes me to shiver a little as my face is flushed and hot from the fire, but my back is cold. I pull a blanket over my shoulders.

The beginning of autumn stirs something inside me I can't explain. The cooler temperatures are refreshing, but they also signal coming changes. Changes that mean the passing of summer, the loss of leaves and blossoms, of fireflies and turtles, hummingbirds and butterflies. Some dying, some hibernating, and some just flying away.

The monarchs, with their orange and black wings, are moving toward the mountains of Mexico once again. The ducks and geese that don't live here the year around will soon be passing high overhead, or stopping for a rest on one of the area's lakes, streams or ponds, as they make their annual pilgrimage to the south.

Insects, reptiles, arachnids, and mammals that sleep through the harsh winters months are making preparations for their long sleep. And even the ones that don't hibernate are trying to increase their stores of body fat to help them survive the lean times.

For the people of the Ozarks this is the time for harvesting the last crops. Many of the fruits and vegetables have already been picked and dried, or canned or frozen, but some apples, along with pumpkins, squash, nuts, persimmons, and even turnips are yet to be harvested.

This is also the time of year when hogs and steers are taken to the local locker plant for butchering, or they are slaughtered and butchered at home. Hunters are starting to get ready for the fall deer and turkey seasons which start next month.

The running water in Long Creek starts to work on me like a lullaby, but I'm not ready to turn in yet, so I stand up, stretch my legs, and decide to walk around. I move slowly away from the fire's light, letting my eyes adjust to the darkness.

I move along the trail that crosses the meadow and goes up the hill to the east. I continue to walk slowly, but as I get nearer to the hill, I notice that my eyes are seeing better in the darkness, and I'm surprised at how easily I'm negotiating the path.

Now and then I stumble or trip against a rock as I work my way up the hill. This would be much easier with a flashlight, but there wouldn't be any sense of challenge.

The sky is looking much brighter now that I'm well away from the campfire, with the stars appearing in the lighter areas above the cedars and scrub oak. The trail continues to wind up the steep hill.

Just as I reach the first rise, near an open glade, the big moon appears through the trees, seemingly motionless, glowing in the night sky.

The moon has always been an object of extreme interest to man. It's been the focus of many superstitions and legends; being given credit for powers and happenings that are purely coincidental. As I look at it glowing so magically, suspended in the air, I have to remind myself that it's really not a light, nor a magical, supernatural sphere; not Diana, Luna, or Cynthia, the Roman moon goddesses; nor is it Phoebe or Selene, the names of the Greek lunar deities. It's just another empyrical body, one-third the size of Earth, that has been caught in an eliptical orbit around the earth, becoming a satellite.

Though I had seen pictures of the moon's surface, it didn't really mean much until the first time I saw it through a telescope. Although it's about 240,000 miles away, there were the mountains and craters, just like in the pictures, but unlike the pictures, what I was looking at was here and now. It was real.

This last statement obviously shows my skeptical nature. Though I didn't doubt the pictures of the moon, they just didn't have the same impact as seeing it "live." I'm sure Neil Armstrong felt the same way. But I doubt that his view of the moon was any more beautiful than mine is right now, standing alone in the Hercules Glades looking up at the big shining ball.

It's strange how it seems to be standing still instead of speeding along on its twenty-nine and one-quarter day orbit of the earth, while rotating on its axis at the same time the earth is rotating at many thousands of miles per hour also. A perfect example of relativity.

Without a telescope, the stark features of the moon are missing. I can't make out the huge craters, some over 200 kilometers in diameter, believed to have been caused by tremendous collisions with meteorites, much less the smaller craters, about one kilometer wide, that may have come from explosive volcanic activities.

I can see the shadows, or darker areas, that have long been associated with a face on the moon, which is called the maria. These areas are thought to be evidence of large lava flows, indicating an earlier volcanic period, much like the earth's.

Charles Darwin believed the moon was originally a part of the earth, and had broken loose and been thrown into orbit. This hypothesis was largely discounted by experiments that showed that physical laws wouldn't have affected such an outcome.

A more acceptable theory is that the earth, and the other planets, accreted from a vast cloud of dust particles, meteroids, and larger asteroidal objects. The objects with heavier metallic content formed the earth, whereas the condensation of more stony objects which weren't as heavy formed the moon. It is still a mystery.

But regardless of how it was formed, or how it was put into orbit around the earth, the moon is obviously there, reflecting the sun's light down on the earth's darkness, turning the Ozark mountains a silvery blue in the soft light.

The Ozark mountains; I've often wondered who named them. I know that the word "Ozarks" came from the French "Aux Arcs," which loosely translated means "to Arkansas." However, I'm not sure why these large hills were called mountains.

The foundation for these hills was the igneous rock which was created by lava flows. When the lava cooled quickly, it formed rhyolite porphyries, or crystals, and when it cooled slowly, it formed granite.

On top of this was deposited sedimentary rocks during the different periods when this land was covered by seas. The rocks left behind were primarily limestone, shale, and sandstone, with deposits of clay and coal mixed in.

It is believed that during the tertiary period, about 65 million years ago, there may have been an imbalance in the earth's crust, which caused this region to be uplifted, pushing the rocks upward to form the Ozark hills.

There are places around the Ozarks where it looks like a cliff wall has been pushed up in the middle, or on one end, making the layers of rock slant at an odd angle. This phenomenon can be seen on Highway 65 a few miles north of Branson, where the highway passes between two cut away bluffs. The bluff on the east side appears tilted on its edge.

With all the rock fractures (faults) underneath this area, I'm surprised there isn't greater earthquake activity here. There have been some tremors in recent years, but nothing like what could, or has, happened.

The greatest earthquake in the recorded history of the U.S. took place at New Madrid, which is in the southeastern part of Missouri, in 1811. Since no white settlers lived in the White River region during the earthquake, there are no records of its effects here, but at New Madrid the devastation was immense.

It began at two o'clock a.m. on Monday, December 16, 1811. In the first hour, most of the structures were demolished. Many reported that they heard the sound of a rushing wind, but no wind was blowing. Trees started snapping, sounding like firing cannons. Deep cracks broke open in the ground, and hillsides and bluffs tumbled into the Mississippi River along a 400 mile length.

Sailors on the river reported that the water spouted up, throwing mud and debris thirty feet into the air. Forests shook like rushes.

The shock was felt over two million square miles, with over 30,000 square miles being raised or lowered six to fifteen feet along the fault.

The old town of New Madrid dropped fifteen feet, falling beneath the waters of the Mississippi. Realfoot Lake in Tennessee was formed when the course of the Mississippi was changed. The lake is now sixty to seventy miles long, three to twenty miles wide, and about fifty to one hundred feet deep.

The river was reported by some to have flowed backwards, and was covered with the wrecks of boats.

The shock was felt in St. Louis, Missouri; Louisville, Kentucky; Cincinnati, Ohio; Boston, Massachusetts; Washington, D.C.; Charleston, South Carolina; Savannah, Georgia; parts of Canada; and as far west as the Rocky Mountains.

Another large shock hit on January 23, 1812, and again on February 7; the last one equal in size to the December 16 shock.

The shocks continued for more than a year, finally totalling more than 2,000. Although this was the biggest earthquake in recorded history, Indian legends told of even earlier disasters in the same area, in the time of their forefathers.

In 1967 and again in 1975, tremors were felt in Springfield, but no serious damage was done. However, scientists believe the New Madrid area is way past due for a major earthquake, and they predict a 50% chance of a quake measuring 6.5 or better by the year 2000.

We are not sure just how much this will affect us in the Ozarks, but with the kind of rock structures underneath southern Missouri, we will feel some effects. Knowing that there are at least fifty faults in the Ozarks region, I'm not about to deny the Ozarks' vulnerability.

I think about the fault, known as the "Ten O'clock Run" by state geologists, that is a stone's throw from my house. It also runs dangerously near Table Rock Dam. I push the next thought out of my mind.

I turn and look toward the meadow where my camp is. This land seems so peaceful and sturdy, so timeless and unchanged. I wonder how I would feel about it if it were to shake, to rise and fall as a wave upon the water, to split open and groan. Maybe it would help me to see it more as another living, changing entity, and not as an inanimate thing.

One of these days the sleeper will awaken.

Starting back down the trail, the moon's light is already lighting my path. I don't have to look as closely at the ground to see the rocks or holes that could cause a twisted ankle.

The trees are starting to cast their shadows as the pale light slips silently through the forest. The meadow is starting to glow as parts of it catch the light.

As the trail reaches the meadow, I get a glimpse of my campfire, flickering through the last stand of trees. It looks out of place with its orange dancing light, while the rest of the glades are bathed in silvery softness.

Nearing camp, I notice a movement near the tent and I stop. The fire's light quickly exposes the intruder, as it reflects off the white and black pelt.

A skunk, or polecat, zorrino, or *mephitas mephitas*, is apparently looking for some food to pilfer. Skunks are quite common in these hills, making their presence known by filling the night air with their odor, or intruding on apprehensive campers, or littering highways as they fall victim to automobiles.

They usually hunt for rodents, insects, eggs, birds, and even some plants, but they aren't above eating carrion, garbage, or anything left unattended. It must have caught the scent of my supplies.

The skunk is a member of the weasel family, along with badgers, mink and otters. Most skunks are nocturnal and terrestrial. The females often have from two to ten babies a year. The babies are equipped just like the adults with scent glands on both sides of the anal opening, capable of spraying the fine yellow odoriferous spray up to twelve feet.

A skunk will often give warning signals, such as foot stamping or hand standing on its front feet, but if one is suddenly surprised, so might be the surpriser. It's hard to believe that the scent is used as a base for perfume.

In the Ozarks, skunks have long been used for fur, as well as food, but I'm not that hungry or adventuresome. The odor of the skunk is enough to make me avoid a confrontation, but they often carry the rabies virus which is a much greater threat, and that makes me even more antisocial tonight.

Quickly picking up some rocks, I throw them, one at a time, towards camp, giving a yell each time. At first, the skunk doesn't seem to notice, but after the third rock and shout, it decides to move off into the darkness and, hopefully, look for a peaceful place to hunt.

But while it's foraging in the night, it will have to stay alert to the danger of ambush from the great horned owl, or coyote, or bobcat that would quickly make it into a meal, but that's its problem.

I move slowly into camp with a rock at the ready in my hand.

The fire is beginning to burn down, but I'm not going to add any more wood. I have a tent and a warm sleeping bag, so the fire is really more of a companion than a necessity. It might have discouraged other wild visitors though, so I'm glad I built it.

The moon is showing through the trees up on the hill, as a nightbird again gives its lonesome call. I listen for a while to the gurglings of the water running in Long Creek, as the dying flames of the fire lick up the sides of the charred limbs. The embers in the heart of the fire glow in a pulsating rhythm. The smoke from smoldering pieces of wood rises straight up into the night sky, and takes on an eerie glow in the moon's silver light as it slowly snakes its way ever higher.

Far off, the muffled sounds of a barking dog echoes through the glades. It's probably a dog from one of the neighboring farms who is on a night foray, and has come across some wild creature that it has chosen as a perfect candidate for harassment. The dog had better hope it's not another skunk.

The moon continues to ease higher into the sky, lighting the meadow in both directions. I take a container of water and pour it over the last visible flames, causing a hissing, sputtering cloud of steam and ash to erupt. The embers react violently to the water that's running through the ashes. Steam and smoke continue to rise from the noisy battle zone.

The brighter stars are still visible in the sky, but the moon's light hides many of the others.

I lay back on my sleeping bag which feels slightly damp from the night air, and look up at the sky. With the nightbird's infrequent call, the bubbling waters of the creek, the distant barking, and the soft moonlight, I feel like I'm lost in time. This could be anytime; last month, last year, a hundred years ago, the day before the big earthquake, or even the time that these hills were first pushed up into the sky. I wonder how many magical nights have glowed just like this one.

My thoughts stop for a moment as the distant roar of a

jet passing high overhead breaks the night's serenity. I catch the movement of its lights as it moves between two of the brighter stars, its lights looking somewhat like stars themselves.

It moves across the sky, finally disappearing behind the ridge to the south, but the rolling noise of its engine takes longer to go away. Eventually the distant roar gives way as peace and timelessness return to the glades.

The magical spell of this moonlit wonderland finally overtakes me, so I slip into my sleeping bag, and zip up the netting on the tent. I can still see the moon through the netting as it forms the image of a moon centered cross.

Slowly, sleep begins to overtake me, and I drift off as the water of Long Creek continues to run in the background of my dreams.

For a little while I will rest, just like the earth and rocks of the Ozarks that lie resting beneath me.

Day Twelve
October 28

Full Circle

A fine misty rain falls through the trees as the clouds hang close to the earth, enshrouding the tops of the brightly colored hills and down through the valleys, causing visibility to be limited.

Here in the Mark Twain National Forest, north of Forsyth, there is nothing moving except the falling mist, and the drops of water dripping from the trees to the carpet of last year's leaves below. Some of this year's leaves are starting to fall, too.

The shortened days and cooler nights, along with a light frost, have slowed the movement of sap from the leaves to the roots, causing the trees to start turning incredible colors, some dappled, some spotted, some streaked, in yellows, greens, oranges, reds, purples, browns, and all the shades in between. Even on this cold, misty day, the leaves are glorious. All around, the brightly colored sumac, poison oak, virginia creeper, elm, hickory, mulberry, maple, oak, ash, and dogwood are on display.

With the colder weather, these woods usually echo with the drone of chainsaws as wood supplies for fireplaces and heating stoves are being restocked. But today, with the falling mist dampening the forest, and making safe footing questionable, all I hear are the droplets of water hitting the wet leaves all around me.

It's only a few more days until the fall deer season opens, so this is probably my last chance to walk these woods and enjoy this year's color.

During deer season, the forests become crowded with hunters, wearing their bright orange hunting clothes, too many of whom are overly eager to make a kill, for whatever personal reasons, and sometimes shoot at shadows or even sounds. And alcohol is too often used to keep off the autumn chill.

It's not a safe place for someone who enjoys tramping through the woods just to see what can be seen.

Walking alone through the damp, brightly colored woods, I feel a great deal of peace. But, at the same time, I also feel a bit of melancholy. This time of color is a signal of change, of going from one season to another, the end of summer, the end of growing leaves, and plants and flowers.

It will be several months before I can again watch new blossoms unfold, or watch butterflies, bees, and hummingbirds stealing nectar, or see tiny columns of ants who are now hiding somewhere underground, or watch bizarre looking caterpillars inching along the ground or up the side of a tree.

It will be a while before I can watch frogs laying their large clusters of eggs along the edge of a pond or backwater pool, or watch the tiny tadpoles swimming around by whipping their snake-like tails.

The terrapins no longer bulldoze their way through the undergrowth, but have burrowed into the earth to hide from the coming winter. So have the frogs and countless forms of insects. And the snakes, too, have slipped off to sleep.

The songs of crickets, and cicadas, and whippoorwills no longer fill the evening, and the call of frogs has turned silent in the autumn air. The only sounds are the drops of water dripping onto the leaves from the trees above.

Looking around at the trees, I wonder at their ages. How many times have they gone through these fall changings and sheddings? How many times have they withstood the onslaught of winter, and sprouted out new leaves in the spring? And what secrets are hidden in their genetic codes, telling of their changes from the beginning?

It's believed that plant life started some three billion years ago in a primordial sea, as tiny green plants. These plants were a form of algae, and at some unknown time, they moved from the sea to land, long before animals made the transition.

Some 400 million years ago, these plants began developing a vascular system which had specialized cells that circulated water, minerals, and food. In the next 50 million or so years, the plants developed roots, stems, and leaves, and also developed a hard, woody tissue which allowed them to grow very large.

And so, about 350 million years ago, the first forests were growing on the earth. These forests relied on spores for reproduction, and they required moist climates to survive.

A little over 200 million years ago, gymnosperms evolved, developing seeds which could survive through dry periods before germinating, but these plants still relied on the wind to carry their pollen.

Some 60 million years ago, angiosperms, or flowering trees, appeared. The blossoms of these trees contained a sweet nectar which attracted insects and birds, who aided in pollenation. As I look at a large oak, I marvel at how simple it appears, but yet is such a marvelously intricate life form. Even now, with its circulatory system slowing down, the xylem, or ringed part of the inner tree is carrying water and minerals up to the few leaves that are still green. And they, through the process of photosynthesis, are creating sugars which are being carried back down the trunk through the phloen, which lies just on the inside of the bark. As the sap containing carbohydrates is carried toward the roots, the tree is fed by way of the vascular rays, which resemble the cuts of a sliced pie, going from the phloen all the way through the xylem to the center of the tree.

But the circle of the nutrients from the roots to leaves, and back to the roots, has slowed greatly from that of summer when it could travel 200 feet in an hour. Now, as the sugary sap has slowed, special cells at the base of the leaves have begun to harden, trapping some of the sugars inside as the leaves die.

The dominant pigment, chlorophyll, which masks the true colors of leaves during the summer, decomposes quickly when the leaves die, and the more persistent pigments, such as carotenes and xanthophylls, remain behind, making the bright yellows and oranges of the elms, hickories, mulberries, and some maples.

But here in this oak tree pigments called anthocyonins are created from the trapped sugars, and cause the burnished reds of its leaves, as well as those of some other oaks and sugar maples. It also causes the purples of the ash and dogwood.

The yellows and oranges start appearing first when the nights grow cooler, but the reds and purples are directly related to frost. Since the first frost has already occurred, the woods are rapidly turning colors, and the remaining leaves on this oak will soon be red. To me, this is one of the most beautiful places on earth.

The United States was extremely fortunate when it acquired this land in the Louisiana Purchase in 1803. Of course, these hills were only a small part of the 2,144,520 square kilometers that France sold to us for $27,267,622, which was less than three cents per acre. This purchase doubled the land size of the United States' boundaries.

If the people of France were walking through these hills right now, I'm sure they would regret the sale. And the Spaniards who came here looking for El Dorado obviously didn't come here during the fall. There is gold everywhere.

Not far beyond the large oak, I come to an exposed rock overhang on the side of a hill. A tiny stream trickles from it to the rocks below; a miniature waterfall. I sit down nearby and listen to the water splatter, while I look around at the dripping forest.

Autumn is a time that creates strong images in my mind. Fields of corn turned tawny by the sun, being harvested by a combine or cut by hand and bundled into shocks, which will feed the livestock, and will also provide shelter for mice, rats, and hibernating snakes. The rows and rows of stubble left behind being frequented by quail, doves, and migrating geese who feed on the stubble and bits of corn they can find.

Large pumpkins lay at the ends of dried, withered vines, ready to be gathered and stored, or peeled and boiled, the cooked pulp made into pies and breads. Or they might be taken to market and sold, or faces carved into them for the upcoming holiday.

Bushels of red Jonathan apples, smelling sweet in the autumn air, eaten on the spot, or cooked into pies, cookies, cakes, jellies, jams, candies, or baked, or made into apple butter, smelling of cinnamon and nutmeg, spread on homemade bread. Or they might be mashed to a pulp in a cider press, and the juice running out to fill jugs and jars that will be put on shelves in a musty smelling root cellar, or it's mixed with sugar and yeast and set behind a warm woodstove, slowly turning it into applejack, good for taking the chill off a body on a cold winter's night.

The sight of hulled walnuts as they lay drying on the porch, ready to be cracked open and the nutmeats picked out, a hammer and broken pieces of shells laying nearby.

A persimmon tree, heavy with fruit that is turning a reddish-gold, now that the first frost has quickened its ripening process, and taken away the alum-like bitterness of the unripe fruit.

Jars of honey, with a piece of wax honeycomb inside, waiting for a hungry dilettante to spread it over hot, buttered biscuits, flapjacks, waffles, or hot oatmeal. Or use it to make jams, candies, or put into cakes and pies. Biscuits and honey and freshly brewed coffee; there's nothing like it.

Open fireplaces, stoked with plenty of dry logs to make a warm, glowing fire, warding off the cold, and at the same time, filling the house with a light smell of wood smoke. As the smoke rises from the chimney, it slows to a stop and then hangs like fog in the cold, moist air of the October evening.

In parts of the Ozarks, bright lights shine down on a playing field as scores of uniformed football players line both sides, prepared to do combat. The stands are filled with fans and supporters from both schools, bundled up, and toting Thermoses, trying to stay warm. The cheerleaders, dressed in their school's colors, try to organize the crowd's enthusiasm into a rallying cry for their champions. This is more than a game, it's a weekly social event, a focal point that brings whole communities together, giving them something to discuss besides politics, or the weather, or religion, or the state of the world. And it allows past heroes the chance to sit and recall their big plays, their days of glory.

Autumn also conjures images of bright yellow school buses driving along country roads early in the morning, picking up blear-eyed kids who try to find seats as close to the heater as possible, while trying to stay away from the door that opens and closes, bringing in freezing air at every stop.

These buses follow the same route every afternoon, bringing the tired, bored kids back home to their evening, before supper, chores; the family dog waiting, wagging its tail at the recognition of a returning friend. Younger brothers and sisters waving at the bus from the front porch.

In Branson, the face of tourism has also changed with the season. During the summer months, the area was full of families, mostly in cars, moving around slowly in the heavy traffic, looking for excitement. Now, with school in session, and the weather more agreeable to the older folks who don't like the heat very much, the area's filled up with many more tour buses and motor homes carrying mostly senior citizens. The go-cart tracks and water parks have closed while the show matinees and craft centers are doing a booming business, this being the month that puts many retailers in the black.

And the lakes are less crowded. The skiers and pleasure boaters have surrendered the water to the serious fishermen.

Although this is a time that reminds me that summer is gone, it's also a time when I realize the advantages of the colder temperatures.

The ticks and chiggers are now hiding under the damp leaves on the ground, waiting for spring. Also, the mosquitoes no longer ambush me while I'm on one of my excursions. And, although 69 of the species of birds and two of the waterfowl that summer here have gone, 37 species are coming in for the winter, and will share the Ozarks with the 51 kinds that make this their permanent home.

One of the incoming migrants is the bald eagle, *haliaeetus leucocephalus*. In 1782, it was declared our national bird, but life has been anything but easy for it.

At one time bald eagles were quite numerous, but wholesale slaughter of the birds by misunderstanding ranchers, as well as professional hunters who were paid bounties by such places as the state of Alaska, which reported 130,000 killed there alone, and also the destruction of their natural habitat, caused their numbers to plummet.

In Missouri, the eagle population was so low by 1900, they had stopped nesting here altogether. Later on, the use of DDT as a pesticide threatened their existance even more, since it washed off farmlands into streams, getting into the food chain, which contaminated the fish that the eagles ate. The DDT caused the shells of the eagles' eggs to be too fragile to survive. Consequently, the American bald eagle became an endangered species.

But with the help of programs such as the Bald Eagle Protection Act of 1940, the eagle population is making a comeback. It is estimated that there are at least five nesting pairs in Missouri, with one pair in the White River region, two in southeastern Missouri, and two in the central part of the state.

I remember the first time I saw a bald eagle in the wild. It was just a few years ago, near Lake Taneycomo. I spent the better part of an afternoon trying to keep the fishing eagle in sight, without disturbing it.

At one point, it seemed to know it was being watched, and it put on a glorious aerial show, flying slowly around and around me in a huge circle. It was wonderful!

This time of year the eagles come back into this region where they'll spend the winter fishing, and preying on the ducks and geese who stay here, before returning to the north country around March.

Watching bald eagles fly, with their white tails and white heads, it's easy to understand why the Indians revered them, giving them the status of gods, or at least, messengers of the gods.

A messenger of Wah-Kon-Tah, the great spirit, the ruler over all, the creator of the wonder, and beauty and splendor of these hills. That is quite a title, and one that the eagle brings honor.

For many centuries, the eagles have undoubtedly come here to nest, or fish in these streams. Sitting high on their tree perches, scanning the water for a meal, or flying, soaring on extended wings, filling the Indians with reverence for the beauty and majesty of these birds.

In their dances and ceremonies, and styles of dress, and even their names, the Indians drew from this grandeur. And not only the eagle, but the bear, elk, buffalo, mountain lion and the wolf.

The Indians learned to respect the wonders of nature, and though not fully understanding its intricacies, attributing many of the happenings to the supernatural, they still lived within the system, seeing themselves as a part of it, rather than a ruler over it, a concept that was brought here by the white man.

The white man saw the Indian's attitude of oneness with nature to be primitive, savage, and inferior. Ironically, the Indian was closer to the actual truth than most people know.

The Indians saw themselves as brothers to the creatures of the forests, even though they knew nothing about the concept of genetics. They couldn't have possibly known that each species has a specific genetic coding, which is a sequence of nitrogen bases in the DNA, *deoxyribonucleic acid*, which provides the instructions for the synthesis of proteins, by determining the sequence of the amino acids that compose those proteins. And that there are four different elements that group together in threes, making up what are known as codons. There are 64 different possibilities of codon formations, which make up the twenty main amino acids, which make up protein. Those same twenty amino acids make up all of the protein used by all of the life on this planet, and the same codons form the same amino acids. The only thing that makes each species different is the genetic coding, or sequencing. In a sense, we are all brothers.

I look again at the water trickling off the rock overhang. The water is coming from the mist that's collecting on the forest and drips onto the blanket of dead leaves below which are slowly decomposing. In about three years, these leaves will become humus, and again be part of the earth.

In this process, they are even now releasing minerals that are being carried off by the water. This water, with a degree of acidity, trickles over the rocks, minutely dissolving the stone, drip after drip, carrying away microscopic amounts to catch pools, or seeping into groundwaters, and running into caves, where it might form stalactites or stalagmites. Or, these minerals may make their way down creeks to streams and rivers, and eventually to the seas, that are even now forming new rock, rock that will someday be a hill or a forest bed. This process is never ending.

The feeling that I sometimes get about autumn being a time of passing is really not true, since these hills have an abundance of wildlife the year around. Besides the many birds who winter here, there are also deer, opossums, muskrats, raccoons, squirrels, skunks, bobcats, field mice, woodrats, wild house cats, stray dogs living in the wild, as well as the domesticated livetock that share this land.

And the lakes and streams still offer their abundance of fish, from trout, bass, and crappie to catfish, walleye and spoonbill.

The Ozarks is a perfect example of nature, ever changing, ever renewing. That which dies is reclaimed and recycled. The cycles of prey and predator always balance out.

When plants increase, so do the herbivores. as the herbivores increase, the plants decrease, and the carnivores increase. As the carnivores increase, the herbivores decrease, and the plants grow once again.

This cycle, the one of plant, herbivore, and carnivore, if unaffected by man, takes approximately ten years to go full circle. Not much time in nature.

The mist begins to get heavier and a light wind moves across the forest, sending the droplets of water accumulated in the trees showering to the ground. Still, there aren't any animals to be seen. This is a perfect refuge.

When I feel a need to get away from the pressures of the outside world, I find a place like this where I can sit or walk, and collect my thoughts. It helps me to put everything back into perspective, and to see how it fits into the grand scheme of things. Usually, when I carry my load of worries into these mountains, they just seem to dissolve, drip after drip, washing away to some unknown seas.

These hills have long offered refuge to man, but not without the costs. The Indians lived for hundreds and thousands of years in these hills, until finally they were forced out.

White settlers also found refuge here, enjoying nature's bounty. But the Civil War raged, and the Ozarks felt its devastating effects, as it disrupted lives and the harmony of these hills. But when the cannons fired for the last time, the leaves fell again, covering the scars of the battles.

After that war, many men returned looking for peace but they found a land of lawlessness, so they banded together, forming the Baldknobbers. This organization was short lived, and failed to bring peace.

And, of course, there were the bushwhackers who preyed upon the weaker citizens, and who used the isolated hills and valleys as a refuge from justice. This had also been the land's appeal to other outlaws, such as Frank and Jesse James, and the moonshiners. Today it's drug dealers, and anti-government organizations. Hopefully these latter intrusions into the peaceful Ozark mountains are also only temporary. It may take a strong public stand to eliminate these problems, but it's a cost with invaluable returns, for this place is priceless.

The abundance of natural resources, such as forest, minerals, water, clean air, and land, make this a perfect setting for the diverse plant and animal life dependent on the availability of these resources.

However, even though there is an abundance of life here, it can all be lost. Without the proper understanding of the delicate ecosystems that make up the Ozarks, one by one these animals and plants can be wiped out, eliminated from the lists of inhabitants. Through abuse and neglect, the riches of the Ozarks that we take for granted may very well disappear. It looks like the gray bats, blind cave fish, cave salamander, pickeral frog, the eastern pepistrelle, among others, may be on their way to joining the list of endangered species in Missouri.

Already on the list are birds like the osprey, double-crested cormorant, sharp-shinned hawk, cooper's hawk, marsh hawk, red-shouldered hawk, least tern, common barn-owl, swainson's warbler; or mammals such as the river otter, and white-tailed jackrabbit; and fish like the lake sturgeon, pallid sturgeon, blacknose shiner, taillight shiner, pugnose minnow, neosho madtom, spring catfish, harlequin darter, and goldstripe darter. The endangered reptiles are the blanding's turtle, Illinois mud turtle, and yellow mud turtle. Of course, the bald eagle is also endangered.

And many on this list are well on their way to joining the wolf, the bear, the mountain lion, and the buffalo who have followed the musk ox, tapir, peccary, as well as the crocodile in leaving these hills.

But, as we have seen with the resurgence of the wild turkey and bald eagle, just as we have abused, so can we correct some of our mistakes. We can begin by learning to respect the delicate balance of life in these hills, and learn to become a part of that balance, like the Indians before us.

Just as we have started to revive the dwindling eagle populations, so can we strive to guarantee the future of all the species.

The bald eagle may very well be carrying a message from God: Abuse and lose, or protect and keep.

These have been a very memorable twelve days. Some have brought great pleasure, while some have brought great pain. But there is not a more perfect place for me to have lived them than in the Ozark mountains. By watching this land go through its changes, from dormancy to life, from life to death, or back to dormancy again. Seeds to plants to flowers to seeds again.

I feel like I understand life a little better, its ups and downs, good and bad, give and take. Much like a leaf, riding along on the currents of a stream that washes down through a valley. It rides over the shallows into still pools, always moving along at the same speed as the water, giving no resistance to the direction it is being taken.

Life is much the same as the water. It isn't to be resisted, but to be experienced, following along on its currents, in the direction it wants to go, and finally being taken to the sea.

I look around once more at the beautiful leaves that hang limp under the weight of the dampness. In a day or two, the sun will again shine down on these woods, and the freshly washed leaves will radiate their marvelous colors against a bright, blue sky.

The birds will again sing in the trees, as squirrels scurry about, busily gathering acorns to store in their tree hollows. A breeze will stir up rustlings through the emblazoned trees, and the autumn's chill will stir some of the later migratory birds to again take to the air on their journeys. But for now, the low hanging clouds have closed in on the land.

The mist has turned into a light rain, and the sound of it falling on the leaves begins to drown out my muffled footsteps as I walk on alone, deeper into the forest.

These are some of the books and periodicals that have helped me to get to know the Ozarks better. I would like to thank all of the people who have worked so diligently to preserve this knowledge, and who have shared it with me.

The Shepherd of the Hills by Harold Bell Wright
Missouri Wildflowers by Edgar Denison
Nature Series - PBS
The Land of Taney by Elmo Ingenthron
Border Land Rebellion by Elmo Ingenthron
The Baldknobbers by Lucille Morris Upton
Harold Bell Wright, Storyteller to America by Lawrence V. Tagg
The Compositae of the White River Ozarks Area by Alice A. Nightengale
Butterflies and Moths of Missouri by J.R. and Joan E. Heitzman
The Fishes of Missouri by William L. Pflieger
Missouri Naiades by Ronald D. Oesch
The Ozarks: Land and Life by Milton Rafferty
Atlas of Missouri by Rafferty, Gerlach, Hrebec
Planet Earth: Forest by Jake Page
Migration of Birds by Fredrick C. Lincoln
Field Guide to the Birds of North America - National Geographical Society
Wild Edibles of Missouri by Jan Phillips
Amphibians and Reptiles of Missouri - Missouri Department of Conservation
Foxfire Series - Anchor Press/Doubleday
Birds of America by Ludlow Griscom
Encyclopedia Britanica
Missouri Conservationist - Missouri Department of Conservation
Ozarks Outdoors
Arkansas Historical

Ozarks Mountaineer
Missouri Historical Review
Missouri Life
Missouri Ruralist
Rare and Endangered Species of Missouri - Missouri Department of Conservation
Missouri Fishes by William L. Pflieger
Field Guide to Missouri Ferns by James S. Key, drawings by Paul Nelson
The Wild Mammals of Missouri by Charles W. Schwartz
White River Valley Historical Quarterly
Marty Stouffer's Wild America by Marty Stouffer
Webster's New World Dictionary of the American Language
Flight of the Phoenix by Helen and Townsend Godsey
Encyclopedia Americana
World Book
Earthquakes in Missouri - Missouri Department of Natural Resources